The *Time Poor* Series
MINDSET

Copyright © 2024   5 Minutes Pty Ltd

All rights reserved. No part of this publication may be reproduced, distributed or transmitted in any form or by any means, including photocopying, recording, or other electronic or mechanical methods, without the prior written permission of the publisher, except in the case of brief quotations embodied in critical reviews and certain other noncommercial uses permitted by copyright law.

Although the author and publisher have made every effort to ensure that the information in this book was correct at press time, the author and publisher do not assume and hereby disclaim any liability to any party for any loss, damage, or disruption caused by errors or omissions, whether such errors or omissions result from negligence, accident, or any other cause.

Adherence to all applicable laws and regulations, including international, federal, state and local governing professional licensing, business practices, advertising, and all other aspects of doing business in Australia, the US, Canada or any other jurisdiction is the sole responsibility of the reader and consumer.

Neither the author nor the publisher assumes any responsibility or liability whatsoever on behalf of the consumer or reader of this material. Any perceived slight of any individual or organisation is purely unintentional.

The resources in this book are provided for informational purposes only and should not be used to replace the specialised training and professional judgment of a health care or mental health care professional.

Neither the author nor the publisher can be held responsible for the use of the information provided within this book. Please always consult a trained professional before making any decision regarding treatment of yourself or others.

Published by 5 Minutes Pty Ltd
Australia
www.timepoor.me

For more information contact:
info@timepoor.me

Book design by Marg Booth
Cover design by Leith Hudson
Edited by Marg Booth

A catalogue record is available from the
National Library of Australia

ISBN - Paperback: 978-1-7637045-0-3
         Ebook: 978-1-7637045-1-0

First Edition: 31 October 2024

DEDICATION

With Gratitude and Appreciation

This book is dedicated to all who are navigating the complexities of living and working in our current busy lives, and who seek continued improvement to live a happier, more fulfilled and contented life.

My gratitude and thanks also to all the wonderful 30 contributors who generously shared their wisdom, passion and dedication to helping others shift their mindset and embrace positive change. Your insights have made this book a powerful tool for transformation.

Special thanks to my wonderful assistant Lauren Finnen whose unwavering support and commitment to every aspect of my work is truly invaluable. Your presence makes all the difference - thank you.

Marg Booth

CONTENTS

CHAPTER 1	Next Level Results	1
CHAPTER 2	Celebrate Small Wins: The Key to Lasting Happiness	7
CHAPTER 3	Boost your MOJO to achieve greater success	11
CHAPTER 4	How to Recognise Work Addiction	19
CHAPTER 5	3 steps to an open and growth mindset	25
CHAPTER 6	What superpower would you like to have?	31
CHAPTER 7	Catch, Check, Change	37
CHAPTER 8	Staying Positive and Optimistic	43
CHAPTER 9	Intelligent Energy Management	49
CHAPTER 10	Five tips to unlearn old habits and beliefs	55
CHAPTER 11	How to Outwit Anxiety	61
CHAPTER 12	Pause Moments	67
CHAPTER 13	Embracing the Art of Slow Living, My Raspberry Summer	73
CHAPTER 14	A fresh look at Mindset	79
CHAPTER 15	Level Up Your Self-Confidence	85

CHAPTER 16	How to boost your brain in 30 seconds	89
CHAPTER 17	Confidence is only a tiny mindset shift away	95
CHAPTER 18	No such thing as a stressful workplace	101
CHAPTER 19	Become the Person and Create the Life You Love with IDENTITY SHIFTING	107
CHAPTER 20	Art for Mindfulness?	113
CHAPTER 21	Brain Tumours, Basketball and Getting where you want to go	119
CHAPTER 22	Mindset Matters During Menopause	125
CHAPTER 23	4 Dimensional Parenting	131
CHAPTER 24	I Can Do This	135
CHAPTER 25	What is 'realistic optimism' and how do I cultivate it?	141
CHAPTER 26	Building a bulletproof mindset	147
CHAPTER 27	Fear Journaling	151
CHAPTER 28	Change Your Thinking to Change Your Life	157
CHAPTER 29	Mindset Secrets of Police Officers and Navy Seals for Civilians	163
CHAPTER 30	High Performance	169

The Time Poor Series: Mindset

Chapter 1

Next Level Results
Scott Greenberg

It's easy to get so caught up in everything that's got to get done that we stop monitoring our thoughts. The problem with that is that our thoughts directly impact the quality of our work, and how well we execute it.

So, if we want to operate at the highest level possible, we need to engage in what I call next level thinking. Here's what that looks like.

My iPhone is a perfectly efficient device. Whenever it receives an input, it automatically produces a corresponding output. If I press the home button, it goes to the home screen. If I type a letter, that letter appears.

What the phone doesn't do is hesitate or doubt itself, or compare itself to other phones. It just does its work perfectly. We human beings are a bit more complicated.

We engage in what I call a trigger to trouble process, which is four stages that very often get us into trouble.

The first thing is we receive input, we are triggered, something pushes our button. It could be a problem or an angry customer. It could be a complaint. Maybe it's an opportunity. It's some kind of trigger, some kind of input that gets our attention.

Then we interpret it. Is it good? Is it bad? Is it pleasurable? Is it painful? Is it an opportunity? Is it a threat?

We recall similar experiences and we start to assign judgment to this trigger, to this event.

Based on our judgments, we then have an emotional response, and after the emotion comes action, or more typically reaction.

Now, we can't stop ourselves as human beings from interpreting our experiences, or from having an emotional reaction.

But that space between the third step, the emotion and the reaction, that's where we get into trouble. Emotionally based decisions usually don't serve us well.

So, what we need to do to think of the next level is to disrupt this process, to take a moment to clear our brains, to get back to a place of objectivity where we can make decisions based on data, based on information, not based on fear, worry or emotion.

The Time Poor Series: Mindset

So how do we do that?

The first thing we need to do is stop looking for solutions, and just step away from the problem.

See, when we experience a problem, the first part of our brain that reacts is the amygdala. That's the part of our brain responsible for our fight or flight response. It's there to keep us safe.

The problem is when the amygdala is active, it blocks the neural pathways to the prefrontal cortex. That's the part of the brain responsible for logic, reason and problem solving. It's the best part of the brain that we need for business or for making any kind of good decision.

So, what that means is that for us to make good decisions first, we've got to chill out. We need to relax our brains so we stop thinking with the amygdala and think with the prefrontal cortex. That's how we disrupt the trigger to trouble process.

So, what does that look like?

For some people it's meditation. They're able to sit and close their eyes and focus on breathing and clear their head. For me, that's not effective. I have a very hard time just closing my eyes and concentrating.

What does work for me is taking a walk, by walking away from my office by disengaging from my problem, it allows my amygdala to calm down, and just being out in the world, seeing the buildings and the people and the plants and trees, calms me down and enables me to access my prefrontal cortex more quickly. Very often that's when I'm most creative, or that's when I see solutions.

Other people clear their heads by writing down their feelings in a journal, or maybe on a piece of paper they'll throw away as soon as they're done.

Other people like to talk through their problems with a professional, or just with a friend.

Honestly, one great resource you have right now is the 5 Minutes for Me App and this book. Spending 5 minutes a day to think about self-improvement rather than just on your problems might be the very thing you need to centre you.

There are a lot of ways that you can clear your head. Figure out what works for you.

The goal is to disrupt the trigger to trouble process. So, if you find yourself really struggling with the situation, take a moment to notice your thoughts and feelings. Then clear your head of emotion and subjectivity so you can make decisions, and take action based on hard data and objective truth. That's the key to internal next level thinking, and the secret to external next level results.

About me

For more than 20 years, I've worked as a speaker, consultant and coach, helping leaders and organisations boost their performance and grow. For ten years, I was also a retail franchise owner in Los Angeles, so I've been in business for a while, and one of the things that I've learned is that busyness is the enemy of leadership.

Scott Greenberg

WOULD YOU LIKE TO FIND OUT MORE?

www.timepoor.me

Notes

The Time Poor Series: Mindset

Chapter 2

Celebrate Small Wins: The Key to Lasting Happiness
Cathy Jimenez

Happy Brain Science: Embracing Small Wins for Lasting Happiness

Today, I have a question for you: What makes you happier—frequent, small bursts of joy or one intense moment of happiness? Science has some interesting insights on this. Research suggests that happiness is more about frequency than intensity. It's the small, happy moments spread out over time that really count, rather than one big, fleeting moment of joy. But why is that? The answer lies in a concept called Hedonic Adaptation.

Understanding Hedonic Adaptation

Hedonic adaptation is a fancy term for our tendency to return to a stable level of happiness despite significant positive changes in our lives. For example, think about driving a new car, vacationing in the Maldives, or dining at that exclusive sushi restaurant you've been eyeing. The initial happiness from these events is real, but it eventually fades, bringing you back to your usual happiness set point.

I've seen this a lot during my time in the corporate world. We often say things like, "Once this project is completed" or "Once I get that promotion, I'll finally be happy." But the satisfaction from completing a project or getting a promotion quickly fades, and we find ourselves waiting for the next big thing to feel fulfilled.

Why Wait? Embrace the Small Wins

What if your next project takes a year to complete? Are you willing to postpone joy until then? If you're waiting for one big thing to make you happy, science advises you to stop waiting. Big, intense moments of happiness don't make as much of a difference as we think, and their effects don't last very long.

Instead of waiting for one grand event, try breaking down your projects into smaller milestones and celebrate each achievement. Savor your progress each time you reach a milestone. This approach not only offers more opportunities for joy but also allows team members to feel satisfaction knowing their project is progressing toward successful completion.

The Power of Progress

Achieving goals and completing projects is great, but we often get so focused on the end goal that we forget to enjoy the journey. This shouldn't be the case. In fact, a brilliant scientist named Teresa Amabile and her team found in their study that simply making progress toward clear and meaningful goals is a key source of happiness for team members (The Progress Principle).

So, next time,
1. Don't aim to get all your happiness in one intense burst. Spread it out.
2. Pursue happiness frequently rather than chasing very intense moments.
3. Remember, it's the small, consistent wins that keep us happy in the long run.

Stay happy and keep celebrating those small wins!

About me

I'm an experienced presenter and facilitator to clients such as Intel, Boeing, and Universal Studios Group, to name a few, and I deliver Happy Brain Science sessions in Asia and around the world. Our mission is to build happier, more engaged teams using a fun, science-based approach to thriving at work.

Cathy Jimenez

WOULD YOU LIKE TO FIND OUT MORE?

www.timepoor.me

Notes

The Time Poor Series: Mindset

Chapter 3

Boost your MOJO to achieve greater success
Mark Zimmermann

I'd like to share some insights with you around the relationship between Mojo, and creating a positive mindset to help drive and achieve your personal and professional goals.

What is Mojo?

To me, Mojo is the word to use to describe the motivation, passion, energy, enthusiasm and drive that flows naturally through us. It's the fuel and essence that enables us to tackle our goals, be ready to take on setbacks and also everything else that life has to throw at us.

I've drawn up seven points that I feel help create Mojo.

1. Start Well
The first one is to always start well.

You'd be surprised how many business professionals, elite sports professionals, leaders and people in general that I've talked to who are really good at setting grand master plans, mapping it all out, and never progressing past the first step. We all need to know that to master each of the stepping stones that lead to milestones and goals, we have to set ourselves up to start well!

Mindset is always key to achieving those steps. Starting well means you will continue well, and give yourself the best chance to finish well.

Part of starting well means that when you're off to bed at night, try and read something that you know will make you feel good. Perhaps you can read your journal entry for the day if it has been a good day, or a funny book you've been saving for a quiet moment. There is great benefit in reading something uplifting, motivational, or listening to something that's inspirational or meditational.

A key reason for getting up on "the right side of the bed" enables and empowers you to accomplish so much more than you normally would. Even if you are not a morning person, if you rise early, you don't place yourself under time pressures, and we all think and act far more effectively when under less time pressures. Hint: focus on making your bed well, each morning. In that way, you have accomplished the first task of the day, and in that way, even if you have a not-so-great day, you will always have a nice bed to climb into...a bed that you have made, with pride.

2. Tough stuff first
Next is to tackle the tough stuff first! Get the biggest and most challenging tasks out of the way as early in the day as possible, otherwise, they will just create anxiety all day. Never shy away

from the difficult things in life. More often than not, the process will reveal it to be less of an issue than you thought it would be. Tough stuff always first!

This will create a sense of achievement and will set you up to smash through the rest of what the day has to throw at you.

Remember, curve balls are part of each day, so we should expect them. Just like setbacks... no journey is without unplanned setbacks - so we must always provision for them. We coach this in the sporting world as well as in the corporate world, so it is no different in our personal lives.

3. Every day is Friday
The next point is to live Monday to Thursday, like it's Friday.

Don't dread the week. Embrace it.

Create fun and laughter around you, as it's infectious and it spreads. So, bring that Friday feeling into your sporting, work and personal life, and watch the impact it has on those around you.

A healthy culture stems from each individual, and your mojo is what drives that. If you hate Monday to Thursday, then chances are you are not living your authentic life.

Don't be on the wrong merry go round! Happiness is a choice. If we are continuously doing the things that bring no happiness into our lives, what are we waiting for to change? We drive our happiness through choices we make.

4. Plan
Next up is to have a clear plan for the day.

How will you know if you are succeeding in winning the day, if you don't have a clear plan for what your goals are for the day? We spoke about those stepping stones.

What are the stepping stones for the day?

I know that it sounds elementary, but you'll be so surprised how many of us fail in this basic discipline.

Prioritise activities that are most meaningful, and aligned with achieving your goals.

There's a great Japanese proverb that I love to quote, which is:

Action without vision is a daydream, vision without action is a nightmare. I apply this through my coaching work in the corporate, sporting and home environments.

5. Bite sized chunks
Next up is bite sized chunks.

Your mojo, motivation and energy are not infinite, so use them wisely.

A daunting to do list can be very scary to look at, and demotivating to tackle, unless you break things down into bite sized chunks. We coach elite sports professionals and those in the corporate world to always break the day into achievable bite sized chunks so that we develop a pattern and pathway of success.

6. Own it
I love this one... next up is own it.

Each day is a gift, so we need to make each day count when it comes to achieving our goals.

Make sure you enjoy and celebrate success. All too often we gloss over the wins.

Likewise, when faced with a challenge, own it, front up to it and deal with it and then move on. Accountability is a trait that earns respect, builds confidence, and creates opportunity.

Hold yourself accountable, and consistently review your goals and progress. Your mindset, energy, passion and your enthusiasm, i.e. your mojo, is the ammunition that you will need to overcome any challenge. Remember, if you are going to own it in the form of accountability, use MOJO as a weapon of mass creation! We see leaders in business and leaders in the sporting arena embrace accountability as a key component to their success.

7. Downtime

Last but not least, I cannot stress how important this point is. Guilt free downtime.

Please make sure you schedule it into each day.

We all need guilt free downtime to help recharge the batteries. Just like any high-performance sportsperson, or anybody who's at the peak of their game - run their race.

We all need downtime to recharge and recover. Our brains are like smart phones with all the apps open and running at the same time. When our phones run out of battery, we plug them in, turn off the apps and leave it to recharge. Our brains and bodies are the same.

We need to stop and recharge so that we can run at full speed again when ready.

I'll leave you with this parting question to ponder:

When it comes to mindset and living your authentic life, what's harder, being incongruent or unaccepted?

One of the most effective tools is the MINDSET MENU that we coach through our MPT Method. If you'd like to explore this more, whether you are a leader in the work place, or on the sporting arena, feel free to reach out and contact us.

About me

Hi, my name is Mark Zimmermann. I'm a Sydney based mindset and performance coach. I'm the founder of On the Mark Coaching an International coaching business with an incredible team of coaches across Africa and Australia. I'm the co-author of Winner's Mindset, an Amazon number one bestseller, and the co-creator of the MPT Method, which brings Mindset, Performance and Team together in a way that enables you to achieve the right balance while performing at your best.

Mark Zimmermann

WOULD YOU LIKE TO FIND OUT MORE?

www.timepoor.me

Notes

The Time Poor Series: Mindset

Chapter 4

How to Recognise Work Addiction
Dr Anneline Padayachee

I'd like to share some key insights I've learnt about work addiction as a recovering work addict.

Every addiction starts with a traumatic experience of some kind, and by trauma, I mean something that causes emotional overload.

For me, it was a racially motivated king punch in 2015. Thankfully, my father was nearby to catch me before my head hit the concrete pavement, but the impact still caused bleeding to my brain and my left eye, and deafness in my left ear for almost two years.

When a person feels threatened (whether that be through an act of violence, abuse or bullying), for most of us in these situations, the aim is to make the threat stop. But if we cannot do that, we actively try to change our emotional state by distraction.

Now, in my situation, I cannot get away from my brown skin. And given that I cannot change my skin (nor should I have to), I chose distraction. While most well-known drugs come in the form of substances that can be abused, addictive comfort eating or addictive behaviours like shopping, gambling, and pornography are just as distracting and problematic.

I never turned to any addictive substances or the usual addictive behaviours. Instead, I held my pain inside, bottled up like a dam. Work, as difficult as it was at the time, was initially just a distraction. It was the one stable thing in my life. I would work until I was too exhausted to have nightmares or panic attacks.

Without realising it work became my safety blanket, but then it progressed to my reason for being. My sense of self became entirely based on what I did and my job title. That's really problematic.

Unlike any other behavioural addiction like gambling or shopping, work addiction is different in one critical way: work is a normal essential activity. It is the only behaviour where individuals typically are required to engage in the activity for at least eight hours per day, at least five days a week.

So, the more work a work addict does, the better it is for the addict because they get their "high" and are rewarded for doing so. It's socially acceptable, it's encouraged, and it comes with some really amazing benefits, like the financial security of earning a good salary, work trips, travel or a company car.

But if you are not aware (like I was not aware) that work is your drug of choice, it becomes a complete nightmare when that work is

The Time Poor Series: Mindset

suddenly taken away from you.

By 2020, my body forced me to take a break. I was really unwell. Even though I was hitched to an IV drip in hospital, I argued with my doctor that I needed to be discharged because I "needed to do my work". In hindsight I cannot believe I even did that. Whilst I understood that it was going to be a slow walk to recovery, my frustration at not being able to work was absolutely maddening.

I ended up in a mental health rehabilitation centre. While I have never consumed alcohol, used drugs or undertaken the usual socially unacceptable behaviours like excessive gambling or excessive eating, during the Addictive Behaviours Group therapy class I realised I was a work addict. The day that information hit me, that knowledge hit me, was the day the walls around my heart cracked open and I could actually explore the unresolved trauma of the racially motivated King punch that led me down this addictive albeit self-destructive path with my psychologist.

I've learnt six key lessons that I want to share with you, so you don't make the same mistakes I did.

1. Mental health affects everyone. If you have a heartbeat and you have emotions, you're susceptible to emotional overload and trauma. This by no means makes the trauma that you've experienced fair or justified. It just means that you have feelings, you're normal and it's ok to not be ok.

2. Emotional distresses left unchecked will ultimately drive you to distractive addictive behaviour. Get help.

3. A drug is anything that is used to distract you from your reality: be that abusive use of substances or addictive behaviours, drugs will ultimately bring you harm in the long term.

4. Work addiction is a very real and often undiagnosed problem. Ask yourself why you do what you do, and if you're doing it to

validate your existence and your worth, you need help. Don't distract yourself further.

5. Every single person is worthy just as they are. Your worth lies in you, and you don't need to prove anything.

6. The 80:20 Rule: Consume healthy nutritionally dense foods, supplement if needed, move every day and sleep seven plus hours 80% of the time, and then be a bit fluid 20% of the time. Looking after your body while you work on your mind and self is essential to coming out the other end whole.

Being aware of these emotional cues has allowed me to become better acquainted with myself, and while I'm back at work again now, I know why I do what I do, and when to turn off.

About me

My name is Dr Anneline Padayachee. I am a food and nutrition scientist who specialises in understanding the complexities of food choices from food producers, as well as their role in providing edible health to the components in food, and how the digestive tract works to extract nutrition from the food we eat.

Dr Anneline Padayachee

WOULD YOU LIKE TO FIND OUT MORE?

www.timepoor.me

Notes

The Time Poor Series: Mindset

Chapter 5

3 steps to an open and growth mindset
Veronica Llorca-Smith

A growth mindset is not only about learning something new. It starts with having an open mind because we can't grow something if it's locked inside a high-security safe.

But what does having an open mindset mean? How do we open our mindset?

The very first step is self-awareness. By nature, humans find comfort in familiarity. We gravitate toward like-minded people, those who are more like us, creating a dangerous narrative of us versus them. We are wired to find comfort in what we know and in things that we are good at. It's called our comfort zone.

However, in order to have an open mindset, we must deliberately create challenges that allow us to lift our anchors and grow way beyond our boundaries.

Here are three stories about how I have applied a growth mindset in my life and in my career.

1. When I was a child, I had to move countries with my family.

By the age of 15, I had already lived in four countries and spoke five languages. I had to make new friends, adapt to new schools, and learn about new cultures, resetting my cultural clock every four years. It was hard, but it gave me the key to unlock my box and paint new horizons.

The more I learned about our differences, the more I was able to remove my cultural lenses and see things differently from a new perspective.

In the early 2000s, I moved to China alone with a brown-leather suitcase and a one-way ticket to learn about the Chinese culture and language and live an adventure. It was daunting and intimidating, but I learned, grew, made new friends, and discovered a new world that was much bigger than my own.

I learned to speak Mandarin, greet people with a gentle bow, and eat with chopsticks.

It was a wild ride. However, taking that risk and betting on the unknown allowed me to open new doors and build a fulfilling career developing businesses and teams across different countries and continents.

2. Public speaking

Speaking in public is daunting, especially for introverts like me. I find comfort in smaller, more intimate groups and one-to-one interactions.

However, when I found myself unemployed during the pandemic, I decided to build my personal brand and expand my area of influence and my digital footprint. I started to speak in public and practiced alone in front of the mirror, worked with a coach, and took every opportunity to grab the microphone and share my message. I took every rejection as a life lesson and kept knocking on new doors. I built confidence, refined my content, strengthened my presence on stage, and became an international keynote speaker, turning my fear into an asset. Courage is on the other side of fear.

3. Learning something new
Think of something that you find difficult and uncomfortable. We tend to learn about things we like and are familiar with. We feel comfortable when we are the expert.

However, when we pick a new topic that is foreign to us, we become a rookie again and we challenge our brain to rewire itself, grabbing new concepts and thinking differently.

We trigger an explosion of stimulation that forces our mind to expand and think bigger.

After years of evading the new digital technologies out of fear and intimidation, I decided to tame the beast and took courses online to study the metaverse, web3, NFT and the crypto world.

By confronting my inner fear with knowledge and education, I managed to embrace the beginner's mindset and evict the imposter who was living rent-free in my head.

These are three very different stories of how to proactively expose yourself to challenges that will help you have a growth mindset and unleash your potential to achieve your goals.

To summarise, here are three tips for having a growth mindset:

Firstly - Be self-aware.
Look inside and identify your own area of comfort, your high-security safe.

Secondly - Seek new challenges.
Don't wait for opportunities to come your way: be a risk-taker and chase them.

Thirdly - Take action.
Take the first step and become comfortable with the uncomfortable.

The Time Poor Series: Mindset

About me

Hi, my name is Veronica Llorca-Smith.

In 2021 I was locked out of my country due to the pandemic and decided to start a new path as a writer and speaker, leaving the corporate world behind.

Since then, I have published 5 books, become an International Keynote Speaker and grown an audience of over 20,000 on social media.

My newsletter The Lemon Tree Mindset has become a Substack Bestseller and my new book, The Anti-Procrastinator will be published by Penguin Random House in 2025.

I turned my passion into my lifestyle and my goal is to help people lift their mental anchors to unlock their potential.

My motto: When life gives you lemons, don't just make lemonade. Use the seeds to plant your own lemon tree - The Lemon Tree Mindset.

Veronica Llorca-Smith

WOULD YOU LIKE TO FIND OUT MORE?

www.timepoor.me

Notes

The Time Poor Series: Mindset

Chapter 6

What superpower would you like to have?
Tony Ryan

What superpower would you most love to have?

This question has been used in conversations for years and often results in some entertaining responses. I've heard everything from turning invisible; or the ability to fly; or having the power to convert anything into chocolate.

Just for now, let's modify the question slightly. In your professional work and your social contribution, what superpower would you most love to have?

Here's why you might need to answer that question to prepare for the dramatic years ahead. Your professional work, and your support for others in greater need, will reshape how we all live on this planet. What you offer with your everyday contribution really matters. So, let's ponder five superpowers you might need in those professional and social support times up ahead.

1. Invulnerability
The first one is invulnerability. In other words, resilience.

Just imagine: no amount of ill-founded criticism would ever affect you.

Here's one significant strategy that near-invincible people often implement. They become more deeply aware of their own thinking. This is important, because what you think about every day is who you are.

Stand back from yourself (sort of as a second person) and observe your own thinking.

This is the first stage to taking ownership of what and how you think.

It means that you then become better at using some decent thinking strategies.

Here's one example of a good invulnerability strategy: imagine using Teflon for the bad thoughts and Velcro for the good thoughts. Let bad thoughts slide off, yet have good thoughts stick to you. The opposite approach is never a good idea.

2. Techno Knowledge
Here's the second superpower: techno knowledge.

This means that you would understand every recent techno advance, and how to apply it in an optimum life context.

Not all, but many technologies actually make life better for you. Oh, yes, they do. If you don't believe that, then try going back and living in the 19th century without washing machines, fridges or mobile phones.

If you understood how to make use of every new technology, then what a superpower this would be. Consider: you would have immediate access to any knowledge you need at any time. You would understand translation systems that enhance global communications. Professionals who combine their humanity with new technologies are going to become increasingly sought after.

3. Wisdom
Here's the third superpower: Wisdom.

Is this a superpower? Absolutely. It's pretty rare, and yet it would enhance your life contribution immeasurably.

You would reach a stage in your life in which you have learned from your mistakes, and have applied those lessons in everyday circumstances. Imagine deeply knowing the best thing to say in the middle of a heated argument, or innately understanding the best course of action in a difficult business environment.

So how do we develop this wisdom? By deeply observing self, by empathically sensing the needs of others, by intuiting constantly, and even by responding with kindness in every circumstance.

4. Immortality
The fourth superpower is immortality.

Your body may not live forever, but your influence through your work will last long after you've gone. A YouTube video will be there forever.

When you engage in future actions and recordings, always remember that they can easily become immortal.

There are endless instances in which your everyday activities contribute to your immortality. Online, it might be a single video interview. In daily life, it might be a single focused 20-minute conversation with a struggling co-worker or with a distraught 15-year-old. These actions can change the lives of others for the better.

This form of immortality is an honour and a service to your community.

5. Predicting the Future
Here's the final superpower: Being able to predict what's up ahead.

One powerful way to predict the future is to continually research your specific field.

Staying up-to-date will help you to develop more effective scenarios in any profession.

Develop newsfeeds (eg. by linking online to outstanding people) who will keep you updated. It prepares you for the unexpected and helps to keep you on track with your life contribution.

Anything that is pure chance cannot be predicted. However, many other things, including your future actions, can be. It's predominantly about your commitment. When you are serious about making something happen, it's more likely that you will put it into action. In that sense, you have predicted what might occur up ahead.

About me

Hi, my name is Tony Ryan and I'm a Futurist. This does not mean that I predict the future. Instead, I help people to prepare as well as possible for what's up ahead.

Tony Ryan

WOULD YOU LIKE TO FIND OUT MORE?

www.timepoor.me

Notes

The Time Poor Series: Mindset

Chapter 7

Catch, Check, Change
Stuart Taylor

I want to introduce you to the 'Catch, Check, Change' strategy.

Some of you may have heard of this already, but I think it's a useful strategy for reflection and reframing during moments when our thinking, emotions, or behaviours aren't really representing us at our best.

The strategy is simple:

Catch
Can I pause and catch some of these negative thoughts and emotions?

Check
Can I check on these thoughts and emotions? Are they helpful or true?

Change
Where necessary, can I change these thoughts and emotions to be more resilient leading to a more resilient outcome?

The research behind Catch, Check, Change is extensive and it's a practical technique that I think is hugely powerful.

It comes from the work on cognitive behavioural therapy, designed and developed by Dr Aaron Beck. When we look at approaches to negative emotion, depression and anxiety, the idea of cognitive behavioural therapy is alive and well. Catch, Check, Change is a derivation of that idea.

When we implement this strategy in our personal lives, it gives us an opportunity to slow down and say: "You know what, the way I'm behaving in this situation isn't me at my best."

In our personal lives, we can look at a specific area—it might be the way we are interacting with our kids, or it might be how we are dealing with doing work around the house or in our relationships.

It's also something we can practice in our work lives. In a work situation, it might be around the idea of getting up to do some public speaking, or taking on a new project or role which might cause a level of panic, concern or worry.

These situations present a great opportunity to use the Catch, Check, Change strategy to help us understand the problematic dialogue and emotions, identify the replacement dialogue and emotions, and practice making that change to achieve a more positive outcome.

Practice pausing in the situation and catching your thoughts or behaviours. Check these thoughts and behaviours to identify whether they are helpful and reflect you at your best. If not, work at consciously changing these thoughts and behaviours to better achieve a positive outcome.

As well as practising the strategy to reflect and reframe our own lives, we can also use it to help others. Can we be listening for when somebody else is struggling with the way they're talking to themselves or the way they're acting? As managers and leaders, we might be able to help others practice the Catch, Check, Change strategy.

Practising Catch, Check, Change to see more consistent results is a commitment.

If you're trying to implement the Catch, Check, Change strategy, the first step is to build in a daily meditation practice.

One of the reasons why we need Catch, Check, Change is because we are running at a million miles an hour.

Daily meditation practice allows us to stop, reflect, have a look at the way we are interpreting our environment and get better at stepping up to a more positive, optimistic approach to our thoughts, emotions, and behaviour.

The next step is committing to the process and taking the time to reflect on your progress in your focus area. Ask yourself each week: "Can I take a minute to check in and assess how this is going?"

The idea of Catch, Check, Change is only one of the many practices we can use to build resilience and learn to master our thoughts and emotions.

The more practice we can get when it comes to these techniques, the more likely we are to achieve a sense of equanimity and happiness.

About me

My name is Stuart Taylor and I am the Co-founder of Springfox, Australia's leading providers of evidence-based resilience training for individuals and organisations. For over two decades, I've worked with a wide range of leaders and teams from organisations including the Royal Australian Air Force, KPMG, Vodafone, and Heinz to accelerate human performance through resilience and wellbeing.

Stuart Taylor

WOULD YOU LIKE TO FIND OUT MORE?

www.timepoor.me

Notes

The Time Poor Series: Mindset

Chapter 8

Staying Positive and Optimistic
Michael Crossland

Many people ask me how I stay positive and optimistic despite the challenges I've faced. I've spent more than a quarter of my life in hospitals. I was part of a trial drug program involving 25 patients worldwide—24 of whom didn't survive. I was diagnosed with stage four neuroblastoma, a cancer of the central nervous system. I had my first heart attack at 12. At 24, I had bacterial meningitis and got fluid on the brain when I was 28. At the age of 32, I was diagnosed with four more tumours in the throat, the following year they found a melanoma on my nose, six months later we had a 11 week premi baby with a horrible blood disease called sepsis and late 2022 six more tumours were found. So, my world has had its fair share of kicks, however I have realised that it's not the adversity in one's life that defines us; it's really about how we deal with that adversity that allows us to lead a remarkable life.

I know we all have a story, a battle, darkness, some sort of pain. But what I think makes us all so different is not so much our pain but our solutions. So, for me, I really have a daily routine that assists me immensely in being optimistic, being realistic, but also being positive towards the challenges that the world throws at me.

So, my three step daily routine which are non-negotiable are: **Activation – Meditation - Appreciation**.

So, **Activation** for me is about getting the endorphins flowing. It's about doing some sort of exercise, whether it's a run, a fast walk, some push-ups, sit-ups, dips, squats, even some star jumps—something just to get the heart beating, to get the adrenaline pumping and to get those endorphins released into our system.

The second step **Meditation** for me has been life-changing, and it allows me to respond to challenges with humility, peace, and gratitude for the learnings behind the challenges before they even present themselves. I thought that meditation was for those that burnt incense, grew long beards, dressed in cotton, and wore no shoes. But I realised now, working with some of the highest-paid professional athletes and some of the most successful CEOs, that meditation is one thing they all have in common. They all understand the power of meditation. They understand that it slows down the mind, and the thought patterns, it enables you to have a greater sense of clarity and a greater sense of peace when the world does throw a challenge at you.

The final step is **Appreciation**. Every morning and evening, I write down in my gratitude journal the three things I am grateful for. I think that if I can ask myself every morning what I'm grateful for, that sets my mind up for a positive and optimistic day. And then if I can ask myself that same question right before I go to bed, that gives me the opportunity to go to sleep with joy, happiness, and peace in my heart. It certainly allows me to get into a deep sleep a lot quicker and I feel a lot more relaxed.

So those are my three daily steps: activation, meditation, and appreciation. I know this stuff is not rocket science and maybe that's why it works for me.

I've learned some really wonderful things in my life. However, I think the most important thing to me is that through great darkness, that is our discovery moment.

We do not discover how unfair our life is, but rather we discover how powerful we have been created. We can't spend our days complaining about the cards that we have been dealt.

I think it's so important that we are grateful that we still have cards and that we're still in the game. We just need to ensure we play those cards as effectively as we can.

Thanks for taking the time to read a little of my journey and I hope it's been able to add a little value to your life. I challenge you each and every day to do something that your future self will be proud of.

Michael Crossland

About me

I'm an ordinary old Australian who's faced my fair share of adversities and now feels very, very blessed to travel the world and share my story with people.

Michael Crossland

WOULD YOU LIKE TO FIND OUT MORE?

www.timepoor.me

Notes

The Time Poor Series: Mindset

Chapter 9

Intelligent Energy Management
Irenee Brooks

Our energy is a fuel for our body, mind and spirit. We can all relate to feeling high or low, even without being fully conscious of our energy levels. By being aware of our energy and strengthening this, we can positively affect our physical and soul well-being.

The last few years we've all had to draw on our resilience to cope with the changes, and a lot of us don't like change. So, we've really had to dig deep and stay buoyant because that's what resilience is commonly thought of as the ability to bounce back after challenging situations.

The HeartMath® Institute definition of resilience captures a newer and broader understanding. "Resilience is the capacity to prepare for, recover from and adapt in the face of stress, challenge or adversity".

Capacity is the key term that is fundamental to resilience.

Capacity is how much of something you have. You can increase your capacity, and accumulate or store resilience, and draw from it when needed. You can think of resilience as the amount of energy you have stored in an inner battery.

It's the amount of energy you have available, and the capacity varies from day to day. The greater capacity and resilience, the greater you are able to maintain your composure and stay in charge of your reactions and perceive things more clearly.

Building and sustaining resilience means becoming more intelligent about how you use your energy and replenish your energy reserves.

There are four main areas of resilience.

You've got your physical, mental, emotional and spiritual, and we have resilience in each area.

Some people are naturally more resilient in one area than another, but each area affects the other. We are emotional beings, and it is the emotional area where we can drain our energy unnecessarily.

Building capacity is the key to enhancing one's ability to self-regulate, just like how you go to the gym to build your physical capacity. It works the same way in every area. You need to stretch beyond your norm and then stabilise at the new level. This is how you build your "baseline" capacity.

We tend to expend more energy than we renew, and if we don't have quality rest, it leads to burnout and health challenges.

The Time Poor Series: Mindset

When you are in a stressful situation, you can't race off to a yoga class or meditate, but you can practice the skills to intelligently manage your energy on the run and recharge quickly.

Like anything worthwhile, you need to practice.

I'm going to introduce you to the first step known as Heart-Focused Breathing.

Focus your attention in the area of the heart.

Imagine your breath is flowing in and out of your heart area or chest area.

Breathing a little slower and deeper than usual.

Find an easy rhythm that's comfortable.

That's it. Simple.

I practice when I'm stopped at the traffic lights.

Studies have shown that when we focus our attention on the area of a particular part of the body, it leads to measurable physiological changes in that area. In this case, it helps shift our heart rhythms into a more coherent state. It also draws attention away from issues which further help our thoughts and stabilise our emotions. The HeartMath® technique called, Heart-Focused Breathing™ creates an inner pause so you can become aware that you have a choice of how you want to respond, without that knee jerk reaction.

When you quiet your mind, you can listen to your heart. And when your heart and mind are in sync, you open to your intuitive self, which will never lead you astray.

HeartMath is a registered trademark of Quantum Intech, Inc. For all HeartMath trademarks go to www.heartmath.com/trademarks

About me

Hi, my name is Irenee. I've been involved with Body Mind Spirit Practices for over 30 years through teaching yoga, meditation and energy healing, and I am a certified trainer of the HeartMath ® Institute Resilience Advantage™ Program, which is used by many people and organisations throughout the world. Intelligent Energy Management is part of the Resilience Advantage™ Program.

Irenee Brooks

WOULD YOU LIKE TO FIND OUT MORE?

www.timepoor.me

Notes

The Time Poor Series: Mindset

Chapter 10

Five tips to unlearn old habits and beliefs
Cristina Dovan

Life gets in the way and at one point; I've been where you might be right now. I was going through a tough time and felt completely lost. I decided to make a change in my life by transforming my mindset. So I became passionate about personal growth and ever since I've worked on overcoming the old limiting beliefs that kept me stuck in a negative state of mind.

That is when I discovered that a crucial aspect of mindset transformation is unlearning. Sometimes the key to personal growth is not just learning new things, but unlearning the old habits and beliefs that hold us back.

Unlearning is an essential aspect of changing your mindset because it involves letting go of old habits, beliefs, and thought patterns that no longer serve you. These fixed habits often form the barriers that keep us from reaching our full potential. To cultivate a mindset that fosters growth, resilience, and positivity, we must first identify and let go of these limiting elements.

Old habits and beliefs are often deeply embedded in our subconscious, influencing our decisions and actions without us even realising it. These can be negative self-talk, limiting beliefs about our capabilities, or unproductive routines that sabotage our progress. By unlearning these detrimental habits, we create space for new, empowering beliefs and behaviours to take root.

Here are five tips to help you unlearn the old habits and form new ones.

Tip number one - identify and challenge limiting beliefs. Start by recognising the beliefs that hold you back. These are often imbedded thoughts that you accept as truth without questioning, these are subtle and difficult to intercept but once you identified what is holding you back, you have to question the validity of these beliefs. Ask yourself, is this true? Alternatively, what evidence do I have to support this belief? Replace these limiting beliefs with empowering ones that align with your goals, otherwise you will be stuck doubting yourself and you will fall back into the same patterns that do not serve you.

Tip number two - embrace a growth mindset. Move from a static mindset where you believe abilities and intelligence are fixed, to a growth mindset where you see them as qualities that can be developed through effort and learning. Changing your mind will help you when things seem daunting. It will be hard but a growth mindset will take you where you need to be. View challenges and failure as opportunities to learn and grow. Embrace the process of improvement rather than just the outcome; it's about who you become in the process not only about the end result. Don't let your circumstances make you believe you don't have what it takes to succeed, grow into the person that will achieve it, work on your skills and improve every day.

Tip number three - surround yourself with positive influences. Your surroundings play a crucial role in shaping your mindset. Surround yourself with people who inspire and uplift you, 'you become the average of the five people you surround yourself with'. Steer clear of negative influence of any kind and be mindful of the media you consume. Engage with content that promotes positivity, growth, and learning; learn from people that are where you want to be.

Tip number four - practice self-reflection and mindfulness. Regularly take time to reflect on your thoughts and behaviours, keep yourself in check, and make sure you process what you listen to and what you read because that's when you internalise it all and only then it will transform you. Journaling can be a powerful tool to understand your internal dialogue and patterns. Practice mindfulness to stay present and aware of your thoughts. This helps you catch negative thought patterns and reframe them in real time.

Tip number five - take consistent action. Start with small, manageable steps towards your goals, don't get discouraged because it seems hard, if you learn everything as you need it you will improve every day, that will make a world of difference. Each small success builds confidence and reinforces your new mindset. Knowing something is just potential power, the true power lies in taking action and being consistent.

Consistency is key to unlearning old habits and forming new ones. Stay committed to your growth journey even when it gets challenging. It's easy to give in to the narrative that we can't control our life, nevertheless we are the creators of our life. Small decisions every day, taking the right action will elevate your life, don't live with the idea that someone outside of yourself can change your life because you will grow frustrated. You, and only you can change your life.

Unlearning old habits and beliefs is a powerful step towards transforming your mindset by identifying and challenging limiting beliefs, embracing a growth mindset, surrounding yourself with positivity, practising self-reflection, and taking consistent action, you can create a mindset that supports your personal and professional growth, and it will place you ahead of the crowd.

Remember, this journey is ongoing, and every step forward is a step towards a more empowered you. Keep striving for greatness, and remember every step you take brings you closer to the person you aspire to be. Until next time, stay positive, stay resilient and keep your mindset strong.

About me

I'm a life coach specialising in mindset and transformation, writer and digital entrepreneur.

Cristina Dovan

WOULD YOU LIKE TO FIND OUT MORE?

www.timepoor.me

Notes

The Time Poor Series: Mindset

Chapter 11

How to Outwit Anxiety
Rik Schnabel

If you think that anxiety is forever or part of your DNA, you are wrong. Anxiety is a learned pattern and it's possible to free from it forever. It was my own anxiety issues and learning how to resolve them that led me to do this important work.

Anything is possible when you untrain your brain of its limits.

I would like to share with you one process to give you a mindset improvement. This should help you to outwit anxiety to help you to become centred, peaceful and calm.

So, let's understand anxiety a little bit better …

The first thing to know is that anxiety is not the beast you think it is. It's not permanent, it's a neurological pattern and with the right tools, you can change a pattern. Any pattern!

Anxiety is a physical response more often due to traumatic events. The brain is like a scanner. It scans for any possible threats to well-being and accesses past memories to seek a solution. When a threat appears, this scanning triggers your thoughts, and your body responds.

A quickening heart rate, shallower breathing, and falling posture are not uncommon. But what is its cause? Anxiety is a learned behaviour. It's a pattern like any other emotion; you can learn confidence as easily as you can learn to be anxious.

Anxiety comes about when you consider a task or an event in the future that in the past you were not able to achieve. It can also arise from something coming up, that in the past, you didn't handle it as well as you would have liked.

Your brain is communicating to your nervous system and putting you on high alert. Just in case your past becomes your future once again. Understand this and accept this as normal. That's right. You are normal. There is nothing wrong with you. You have merely learned an anxiety pattern.

One thing you must know is that your thoughts are not always right, and your brain just does what it thinks you want it to do.

Did you know that you can outwit anxiety by doing a few simple things?

I would like you to measure your anxiety right now from zero to one hundred.

The Time Poor Series: Mindset

Zero means you're not anxious at all, and one hundred means you're at the peak of anxiety. Now, if you're not at the peak of anxiety, you're not at one hundred. If you don't have any anxiety at all, then you're not zero either. Then you must be somewhere between zero and one hundred.

Give yourself a score now without thinking too much about it.

The first thing to do is to stop thinking about the future or the past. Bring your mind to the present.

We know that your brain likes to be busy. So, focus your entire attention on your breathing. Slow down your breathing and deepen your breaths, all the way down to your stomach.

Take slow, deep, six second breaths in, and slow and deep, six second breaths out. Do that for one or two minutes.

Now, while you're breathing like this, this balances out your sympathetic and parasympathetic nervous system. Fast and shallow breathing typically signals your amygdala in your brain to fight-flight – which means to run, to fawn – which means to comply or quit, or to freeze.

Now, regardless if you are sitting or standing, straighten up your spine slightly, lift your chin and you should notice your confidence increase. Albeit slightly.

The next thing I would like you to do is while your chin is slightly raised and your spine is nice and straight, just start breathing in six-second cycles to calm your sympathetic and parasympathetic nervous systems.

Count to six - Breath in
Count to six - Breath out
Breathing in, now breathing out in six second cycles.
Breathing in, now breathing out.

Now, I would like you to remeasure your anxiety right now from zero to one hundred.

Zero means you're not anxious at all, and one hundred means you are at the peak of anxiety.

Give yourself your new score now without thinking too much about it.

If your number went down, so did your anxiety.

If it didn't, continue the six seconds cycle of breathing until it does.

That should make a difference. If your anxiety doesn't reduce or go away, then there is something going on at a much deeper level. Your brain is responding to a trauma of the past - even if you don't have any conscious awareness of it. If this is the case and you need more help, here is the link to book your free session here: https://lifebeyondlimits.com.au/help/ By booking using this free help link, one of our experts will provide you with more advice or help.

About me

Hi, my name is Rik Schnabel and I am Australia's Brain Untrainer with Life Beyond Limits. Since 2002, I have coached and helped thousands of people stop their anxious patterns. I help my clients to dissolve anxiety, depression, and many other neurological issues.

Rik Schnabel

WOULD YOU LIKE TO FIND OUT MORE?

www.timepoor.me

Notes

The Time Poor Series: Mindset

Chapter 12

Pause Moments
Jem Fuller

I'm here to share with you a beautifully simple, yet powerful practice, that can become your way to recalibrate and return to your internal state of calm centeredness—your place of equanimity. This exercise can easily become a part of your day.

The Inspiration Behind the Practice
I was first inspired to create this practice in 2014 at the Global Mindful Leader Forum in Sydney, Australia. One of the keynote speakers was a meditation teacher from America. Although he was small and unassuming in stature, he emanated such a beautiful and gently powerful presence. As he walked across the stage, the

auditorium became completely silent—a pin drop moment. In his hour of sharing wisdom with us, he said two things that stuck with me and have since become habits.

One was, "Know the work, but DO the work." He was referring to meditation. It's one thing to understand meditation and sometimes sit; it's another to create a dedicated and consistent practice. That was the time I committed to a regular, habitual practice.

However, it was the second inspirational thing he said that I want to share with you here, and I hope you choose to adopt it. He simply said, "Pause often." I contemplated this and took the instruction quite literally. From that day, I set about creating a habit to pause several times throughout the day. I call them 'pause moments'—just a few seconds to stop what you're doing, notice what you can notice, and then continue.

Implementing Pause Moments
Pause moments are a form of mindfulness—a brief observation of the present. During these moments, you scan whatever shows up in your conscious awareness. Over time, as you create a habit of pausing and noticing, you will develop the ability to easily and quickly shift your physiology (your emotional, mental, and physical state), returning to your centre of calm clarity.

I find these pause moments helpful when you are in between tasks or on the way somewhere. For example, when you've just finished something at your desk and you're on the way to put the kettle on —pause, check-in, and then continue. Pause moments are especially effective when you're running late for an appointment. After your pause moment, you're only five seconds later than you were going to be, but you arrive in a different 'state of being'.

The Benefits of Pause Moments
I am passionate about improving our functionality as individuals and the positive impact that has on us collectively. Our ability to more consciously communicate, collaborate, and create solutions together

is enhanced. Often, we're caught up in our ego and our identification with the experiences of our waking moments. We identify with our thoughts, emotions, beliefs, and ideologies. We judge others and hold rigid expectations of how we think things should be.

By teaching ourselves to pause, breathe, and simply notice with less attachment, we create little reminders that we need not always be driven by our ego. This makes us much more effective communicators and enhances our relationships in all areas of life.

Creating a Habitual Practice
If you are interested in creating your own habitual practice of pause moments, here is an effective habit-forming hack: link the new habit you want to form with an existing habit. For example, brushing your teeth. You already do this probably twice a day. Just take a sticky note, write the word "pause" on it, and stick it on the mirror by your toothbrush. Every time you go to brush your teeth, pause and do a mindfulness scan. Over time, you will create a neural association and won't need the sticky note anymore. Each time you reach for your toothbrush, you will automatically pause.

You can do this with many actions: making a cup of tea, sitting in the car before turning it on, opening your sock drawer, and so on. Initially, you might have sticky notes all around the house, but after some time, you will have created your new habit and won't need the notes.

Perhaps after reading this, you might pause and just notice what you can notice—your breathing, your heart rate, your bubbling thoughts—just for a few seconds. I hope you enjoy creating habitual moments to pause and 'smell the roses'.

Thank you for taking the time to read this. I wish you more tranquillity and moments of calm.

About me

I work as a mindset and communication coach with leaders in the public, private, and not-for-profit sectors.

Jem Fuller

WOULD YOU LIKE TO FIND OUT MORE?

www.timepoor.me

Notes

The Time Poor Series: Mindset

Chapter 13

Embracing the Art of Slow Living, My Raspberry Summer

Gail Gibson

Being presently present is a personal goal I've been mastering for many years. Over the past year, I've elevated my commitment to purposefully cultivating presence through practice, self-reflection, and feedback. My daily practice of becoming more present has proven to be a deeply intentional and fulfilling experience. I've learned more about myself and others by being curious, listening deeply, and giving 100% permission to be engaged in whatever I am doing, whether I'm writing, coaching, in conversation, or walking in nature.

As an accredited Master Coach for women leaders - practice,

self-reflection, and feedback sit at the heart of my work. I inspire resilience, helping leaders break through barriers and conquer challenges with determination. I'm renowned as a game changer for countless women leaders globally, empowering them to find their voice, lead with confidence, and thrive.

Nurturing well-being through nature, I find inspiration in the simple things, and I bring that sense of calm and focus to my work. During client coaching calls, I've upleveled my engagement commitment by setting a 90 over 10 goal to listen as deeply as I can 90% of the time, and talk 10% or less. A determined work in progress with proven results leads to better outcomes for my clients.

Over the summer, I'm morphing my intention for slow living. When you slow down the pace of life, you start to experience everything around you on a more conscious and connected level. With eyes and ears wide open, your surroundings amplify. It's an incredible experience to slow down your mind and your body and surrender to embracing the art of slow living.

I'm delighted to share one of my summer joys: picking raspberries in my garden. The precious gift of Mother Nature's bounty delivers such a wonderful harvest. What I enjoy most is making raspberry picking a daily habit. For me, this is a time to step outside, away from work, and interconnect with nature. Picking raspberries is a daily activity I look forward to, feeding my curiosity, each experience is an adventure because I never know where some of the raspberries are hiding. Going slow and picking raspberries is such a joyful habit which makes me smile every day. What I'm learning most from the experience is to savour the moment, to give myself permission to connect with myself, spend time in silence, and connect with the act of raspberry picking. With gracious thanks to Mother Nature for her bounty, I enjoy the fruits of my labour, paying it forward by making and sharing delicious raspberry and vanilla jam with friends, or simply enjoying a bowl or two of fresh raspberries with cream.

The Time Poor Series: Mindset

What gives you the most joy when you make time to savour the moment?

A great place to start slowing down and getting into the moment is while you're brushing your teeth. As you brush, slow down your strokes and focus on gently brushing each tooth with care. When you rinse your mouth, feel the sensation of the water slowly.

When you find your joy moment, reflect on these questions:
How did you feel being in the moment?
What did the time do for you?
Which senses were sparked?
How did the moment refresh your thinking?
Did the moment gift peace and calm?
How will you commit to practicing the daily habit?

As the season continues, so too does my practice of being presently present and embracing the art of slow living. Nature abounds with colour and change. I can feel the wind, smell the rain, taste the berries, listen to the feathered chorus, and watch new growth.

About me

I am an accredited master executive coach, mentor, author, and podcast host. My coaching style, empowers women leaders worldwide to break through frustration and achieve fulfillment, sparking profound personal and business growth.

Gail Gibson

WOULD YOU LIKE TO FIND OUT MORE?

www.timepoor.me

Notes

Chapter 14

A fresh look at Mindset
David Penglase

Here I am sharing with you some evidence-based research, tips, and strategies around the impact your mindset can have on your capacity to flourish – both personally and professionally.

As a behavioural scientist, I've been fascinated for most of my adult life, both academically and experientially, about what causes people to think, feel, and act the way they do. In other words, I'm fascinated by our mindsets and their impact on our potential to flourish.

There is a lot of self-help nonsense around mindset, the power of

positive thinking and manifesting. I was once told by another behavioural scientist, George Dudley, to watch who you let near your mind – good advice when it comes to understanding mindset.
You may hear motivational gurus tell you that you can simply choose your mindset.

In fact, science does validate if you're already positive and optimistic, when you experience difficult situations, you will more than likely have the potential to snap yourself out of any difficult thoughts or feelings, choose a positive mindset, and take positive action.

But what science also validates is that approach does not work all the time, even for positive, optimistic type people.

If you are not a naturally optimistic person, and you try to choose a positive mindset by doing battle with difficult thoughts to make them more positive, you will more than likely simply amplify the difficult thoughts and feelings and end up feeling worse because you couldn't rid yourself of that negativity.

So, what's an alternative to trying to choose your mindset, especially in difficult times? Here's what we know from a vast range of evidence-based research.

First, overwhelm is a sense of being out of control and one of the biggest contributors to stress and mental health issues in the workplace.

If you're feeling a little overwhelmed, one proven strategy is to use your personal values as a guide to choose goal-supporting actions and behaviour.

The problem is, few people are clear about their personal values and therefore lack a key resource required for them to flourish, both professionally and personally.

The Time Poor Series: Mindset

In pressure environments or difficult times, it can be so easy to get stuck on difficult thoughts and feelings and base your decisions and actions on them.

Whereas, when you're clear on your personal values, regardless of difficult thoughts and feelings, you're more able to accept and detach from them, which frees you to make better decisions and take more positive goal-supportive actions.

Here is a powerful and evidence-based question you can practically apply in difficult times:

With this decision I'm about to make or this action I'm about to take, is it aligned with my personal values, and will it move me toward or away from being at my best and flourishing in life?

Your thoughts are just thoughts, and your feelings are just feelings. Regardless of what you think or feel, you can choose to take appropriate and positive action.

While it's great if you can choose to have a positive mindset, what's more important is choosing to make appropriate decisions and take appropriate actions.

About me

I'm David Penglase and I hope you enjoyed and found value in this chapter. For now, my very best to you.

David Penglase
Behavioural Scientist
B.Bus(HRD), MBA, MProfEthics, MScAPP.

WOULD YOU LIKE TO FIND OUT MORE?

www.timepoor.me

Notes

The Time Poor Series: Mindset

Chapter 15

Level Up Your Self-Confidence
Anthony Ikin

Building confidence has been a lifelong journey for me. As a teenager, I faced intense bullying. Every day at high school, I was called names like "gay" or "faggot" or "poofter." Whether I was walking to the tuck shop or sitting in a math class, the insults were constant. I couldn't understand why people hated me just because I liked different things. But deep down, I had a confidence that kept me going. That inner strength led me to amazing places. I performed as a soloist at the Moulin Rouge in Paris, reached the top 20 in the first season of Australia's So You Think You Can Dance, and even became a world aerobic champion. If I had let the bullies derail me, none of this would have happened.

Now, I want to share some tips that have helped me so you can boost your self-confidence, too. These steps are simple and free, and you can start using them right away.

1. Tell That Negative Voice to Get Lost
We all have that nagging voice in our heads that says we're not good enough, don't deserve success, or will fail. Even the most successful people experience self-doubt. The difference is, they recognise that voice and shut it down before it takes over. So, when that negative voice starts talking, tell it to get lost and focus on what you set out to achieve. The voice may never go away completely, but you have the power to decide whether to listen to it or not.

2. Smile More
Smiling, even when you don't feel like it, can make a big difference. When you smile, your brain releases neurotransmitters that promote a positive emotional state. This happens even with fake smiles! So, make an effort to smile more. It's scientifically proven to help you feel happier.

3. Celebrate Others
Pay attention to how you talk about others because it reflects how you talk to yourself. Wish success for others and celebrate their achievements. If you harbour bitterness towards someone else's success, you'll attract more bitterness into your life. There's a saying I love: "Give the energy you wish to receive." If you want more success, celebrate others' success. If you want more self-confidence, use encouraging language with others. Give the energy you wish to receive.

In Summary:
- Tell your negative head voice to get lost.
- Smile more.
- Genuinely celebrate others.

By following these simple tips, you can start building your

self-confidence today. Remember, it's a journey, and every step you take brings you closer to the confident, positive, and happy person you want to be.

About me

I'm a life coach who specialises in self-confidence, positivity, and overall happiness. I also travel the world as a keynote speaker, sharing this message with people everywhere.

Anthony Ikin

WOULD YOU LIKE TO FIND OUT MORE?

www.timepoor.me

Notes

The Time Poor Series: Mindset

Chapter 16

How to boost your brain in 30 seconds
Dr Helena Popovic MBBS

Most people work on building up and boosting their financial assets. But how many people work on building up and boosting their greatest asset: their brain?

The revolutionary field of neuroplasticity has shown that we can change the very structure and function of our brain. We can grow new brain cells, new circuits and new connections in response to what we do, how we think and the way we respond to daily demands.

We are more than passive victims of our genes, our past or our circumstances; we play an active role in how our brain develops and operates throughout our life. However, most people are yet to realise the enormous personal power this gives them. When we discover how to boost our brain, we boost our performance, productivity and resilience in every area of our lives. In addition, we can more than halve our chances of ever developing Alzheimer's and other dementias in later life.

So how can we start to boost our brain right now?

Brain Booster #1
Get moving.

Yes, yes. We all know we need to exercise 30 minutes a day to stay healthy.

But even 30 SECONDS makes a profound difference to our brain. Yes, that's right, you haven't misread.

Thirty seconds of running as fast as you can — whether it's on the spot, along a corridor or up and down stairs — or 30 seconds of fast pedalling against resistance on a bike, or 30 seconds with a skipping rope, gives your brain a burst of oxygen, energy and most importantly, a chemical called BDNF, which stands for brain-derived neurotrophic factor.

BDNF is a neurotransmitter — a protein that stimulates the growth of new brain cells (neurogenesis) and new connections between brain cells (synaptogenesis).

This means our brain operates at its best in the first hour after engaging in any form of physical exercise. A German study found that 20 minutes on a treadmill boosted language learning by 20%. A Japanese study found that 20 minutes on an exercise bike improved creativity and problem solving. But as I said, even 30 seconds of movement improves our mood and immediate brain performance.

So before anything mentally taxing like an important meeting, job interview or IKEA furniture assembly, get breathless for 30 seconds and you'll perform measurably better. Obviously, if you haven't exercised for a while, build up to full intensity. But the message is: anything that raises our heart rate also raises our cognitive functioning.

Brain Booster #2
Get a 'Can Do' jar, not a candy jar.

Find an empty glass jar, write down the words 'CAN DO' in capital letters on a piece of paper, and stick the label to the jar.

Neuroscientists have discovered that we can boost our creativity and problem-solving ability by removing the word 'can't' from our vocabulary.

The human brain responds to everything we think and say as though it were an instruction or a set of commands. Therefore, the word 'can't' has the effect of giving our brain a restraining order or putting our brain in a straitjacket.

One word can shut down our ability to find solutions because we don't see with our eyes, we see with our brain. We see through the filter of our beliefs, expectations and self-talk.

For example, if I predetermined that I can't do something, I shut down my ability to see how it can be done. I won't notice if an opportunity presents itself that would help me solve the problem. A solution is simply not on my radar. This is known as 'mind blindness'. Our brain absorbs what we tell ourselves and acts on our inadvertent directives.

Thus, we would all do better to cut out the word 'can't' from our vocabulary. That's where the 'Can Do' jar comes in. It's a visible reminder of the power of language.

Every time you catch yourself saying or thinking, 'I can't do this' or 'it can't be done' or one of the many euphemisms for 'can't' such as 'it's impossible' or 'I'm too old for this', put a gold coin in the glass jar. And when the jar is full, donate the money to your favourite charity.

This makes the whole exercise a win-win situation because you're helping the charity achieve their goals.

By doing good for others, we also boost our brain function by releasing a cocktail of feel-good chemicals and delivering more blood to our prefrontal cortex — our higher centres of reasoning. This has been demonstrated on MRI scans.

The goal, of course, is that after a while your jar will remain empty because you've broken the habit of self-sabotage.

Brain Booster #3
Get curious.

Albert Einstein said of himself: 'I have no special talents. I'm only passionately curious.'

Curiosity activates multiple regions of our brain involved in memory, creativity and problem solving.

Whenever you feel like saying the word 'can't', swap it for the word 'how' and ask a constructive question. Instead of saying, 'I can't do this', ask yourself: 'How can I do this?' Instead of saying, 'I can't get the kids to eat vegetables' ask: 'How can I get the kids to eat vegetables?'

Asking 'how' is more powerful than repeating affirmations because you're programming your brain to search for answers. You don't have to consciously try and work out the solution. Just ask the question and go about your day and your brain will work on the problem beneath your conscious awareness. Before you know it, the solution will pop into your head or present itself one way or another.

Try it. It feels like magic, but it's simply the power of your subconscious mind.

So: Get moving
    Get a can-do jar
    Get curious
    And get into reading my books!

About me

Dr Helena Popovic MBBS is a medical doctor, international speaker, and Australia's leading authority on improving brain function. She is also the author of three best-selling books about the brain, dementia, and shedding excess body fat without dieting, drugs or deprivation. Her driving philosophy is that **education is more powerful than medication** and she believes in slow ageing despite fast living.

Visit drhelenapopovic.com to discover how to:
• Boost your brain at any age or stage of life
• Stay as sharp at age 90 as you were at age 30
• Live longer, stronger, healthier and happier.

Dr Helena Popovic MBBS

WOULD YOU LIKE TO FIND OUT MORE?

www.timepoor.me

Notes

The Time Poor Series: Mindset

Chapter 17

Confidence is only a tiny mindset shift away
Sinead Sharkey-Steenson

As a leadership career coach for women, I love helping women build the confidence they need to pursue the careers they desire, particularly in leadership roles. Confidence and self-belief are the cornerstones to achieving your true potential, yet so often are what holds us back.

I've personally experienced low points in my career where my confidence and self-belief were severely lacking. I remember sitting in meetings feeling completely out of place, which of course prevented me from speaking up. I'd get so frustrated with myself, but struggled to shift my thinking. You see I was focused on all the reasons I wasn't enough, on all the things I thought I couldn't do, and on everything I believed I was missing. Instead of recognising the valuable contributions I could make, I doubted myself.

The tips I want to share with you are designed to help you build confidence and self-belief through simple practices. These practices have shifted me from being nervous in challenging situations to recognising that I am important, that I have something valuable to give, and that my contributions are worth sharing. This transformation from fear and nerves to confidence is incredibly empowering.

Focusing on What You Have
When we lack self-belief and our confidence is shaky, we often focus on the wrong things. You're pointed in the complete wrong direction. You're looking at all the gaps that you perceive you have, when actually what you need to do is turn yourself around and look within and see what is it that I do know in this situation? What can I bring to this situation? What knowledge or experience do I have that's like this? And how have I dealt with something like this before?

When you start to focus on what you have instead of what you feel you're missing, things look very, very different, and you can start to build that inner self-belief muscle. To build that inner self-belief muscle, think of it as a core muscle in your body that you're exercising and growing. As it gets stronger, you become more confident, which is the outward projection of self-belief, enabling you to tackle more challenges.

Steps to Build Confidence

Catch and Redirect Negative Thoughts: Notice when you're doubting yourself. Acknowledge that you're focusing on the wrong things. When you feel small, weak, or overwhelmed, notice that feeling and recognise it as a feeling. It's not a fact. Take a deep breath and ask yourself, "What do I know? What can I do in this situation?" Redirecting your focus from what you lack to what you have is the first step in building confidence. And if you simply add the word 'yet' into your vocabulary, you can acknowledge what you don't yet know as a learning opportunity...

I know x/y/z about this, and I know I'm not comfortable with a/b yet, but I know from experience I will learn this and get better and better!

Practice Gratitude: Growing your confidence can be further supported by practicing self-gratitude. Keep a gratitude journal and regularly write down what you're grateful for, this helps with your shift in focus from what's missing to what's there. Ask yourself daily, "What did I do well today? How did I add value? How did I contribute today?" This practice helps build the neural circuitry in your brain to notice your strengths and contributions, reinforcing your confidence.

Reframe fear: The third thing you can do is to recognise that when you feel nervous or afraid, then it means you care about the outcome. Caring is a great thing! Caring means it's important to you, therefore it's something worth paying attention to. Instead of getting sucked into the fear, what you can do is recognise that the fear is a message to pay attention...so fear can actually be your friend. Ask yourself, what's really going on? Am I afraid because this is an exciting opportunity? You can thank yourself for helping you recognise it...and reframe those nerves to excitement instead. So bringing it all together you can change your self-talk to this...

I'm excited to have the opportunity to do this new thing, I may not have done this before but I've done x/y/z like it before, and what I don't know yet I get to learn!

So, go forth, believe in yourself, and know that you've absolutely got this.

Sinead Sharkey-Steenson

About me

Sinead Sharkey-Steenson is a Leadership Career Coach for women, helping women to confidently step up and lead with impact. Since starting Generation Women she has supported close to 10,000 women to step up and make big things happen in their careers.

Sinead Sharkey-Steenson

WOULD YOU LIKE TO FIND OUT MORE?

www.timepoor.me

Notes

The Time Poor Series: Mindset

Chapter 18

No such thing as a stressful workplace
Darren Fleming

You may not be feeling it right now, but there's no such thing as a stressful workplace.

Hear me out on this.

If the environment causes the stress, it will affect everyone in the same way.

An example of an environment causing the stress is boiling water. If we both put our hands into boiling water we will both get burned. We both react the same way to the environment. Workplaces are not like that - everyone responds differently to the environment. Some thrive, others not so much.

My beautiful friend Pollyanna loves skydiving. To me it's terrifying. If we were both standing on the side of a plane at 10,000 feet, she'd be excited and ready to jump out while I'd be terrified and ready to pass out. If we're standing side by side and having different reactions it is clearly not the environment that is causing the stress; it has to be something else.

So what's causing the stress?

How we engage with the World
We interact with the world through our six sense organs of sight, sound, taste, touch, smell. The sixth sense organ of mind detects cognitions that are occurring in our brain.

All sense organs are processed by the brain. For the body to know what is happening, the brain needs to send a signal to the body. This is done in the form of a sensation. It is the way we react to the energetic sensations in our body that cause us to think there is stress or not.

Back to my friend Pollyanna. She looks out across the world from 10,000ft and receives the sensory input. From previous experiences her brain assesses this sensory input as a desirable situation and sends a sensation to the body that encourages her to jump. My brain on the other hand assesses it differently. It uses the same sensory input and my previous experiences to assess the situation as one that is not desirable. As a result my brain sends a signal to my body that encourages me to get out of the situation (which is why I have never tried skydiving!)

Two quick steps to Liberation
If the stress we experience is not caused by where we are, but our reaction to it, we can eliminate stress in our life with two quick steps. Knowing this is the most liberating piece of wisdom we can find.

Lose the labels

The first step is to stop labelling what you are experiencing. You are not experiencing stress, frustration, anger etc. You are experiencing an energetic sensation in your body. You have put the label on it.

When you label a situation as stressful you bring in memories of all the other times you have felt stress. You then have to deal with the sensations from these times now. This only serves to compound the problem you are dealing with.

By labelling you increase the intensity of the sensations from the current situation. This doesn't help you get through what you are dealing with.

Pay Close attention

Pay 100% close attention to the energetic sensations you are experiencing. When you do this, the energetic sensations will change, and in a short period of time, it will dissipate. When it does it will be gone and you won't have to deal with it.

This is what the Stoics meant when they said the obstacle is the way. It's the truth behind the old saying, what you resist persists. Stop resisting what you are experiencing. Experience it fully and it will go away taking the stress with it.

So the next time you are experiencing sensations in your body that used to cause you to think that work is stressful, just pay 100% close attention to what you are feeling. Drop the labels and just experience what is happening. When you do, the sensations will change and the story of stress will fall away. You will then be able to deal with what is in front of you.

About me

Sitting in silence for 10 days straight taught Darren more about the human psyche than his three-year psychology degree and studies in philosophy ever could. It provided deeper insights into performing under pressure than his 10 years of sailing for Australia.

The author of seven books on communication, sales and leadership, Darren's latest publication 'Mindset Mastery: Do less. Achieve more' has been translated for the Japanese market. He travels the world showing others how they can re-train their mindset to be less reactive, less stressed and more peaceful.

Darren Fleming

WOULD YOU LIKE TO FIND OUT MORE?

www.timepoor.me

Notes

The Time Poor Series: Mindset

Chapter 19

Master Identity Shifting: Transform Yourself and Create the Life You Truly Love

Hedi Schaefer

Why Identity Shifting?

Identity shifting is the process of transforming your self-concept to align with your desired life. Why is this practice crucial? Because our identities shape our thoughts, behaviours, and ultimately, our realities. As an example: If I believe that I can live at the beach, home schooling, while making tons of money by doing the things I love, my actions will move me towards that dream. If don't believe it, the dream will stop right that second.

By shifting your identity, you can break free from limiting beliefs and patterns that have held you back your entire life, enabling you to step into your full potential and live a life of fulfillment and success. This transformation isn't just about achieving goals; it's about becoming the person who effortlessly attracts and sustains those achievements. When you shift your identity, you create a foundation for lasting change, where your external world begins to mirror the empowered and authentic self you've cultivated within. Makes sense?

To become the person and create a life you love, you have to shift your identity. Most people are living in self-doubt, anxiety, shame, negativity—you name it. They are not living their full potential, power, and purpose. And that is simply put: a tragic waste of human potential. Because everyone has a gift and everyone is here to experience and give away this gift to the world. This is what I believe wholeheartedly.

A Little Example: My Journey to Identity Shifting

I was traveling the globe, living an innovation consultant life, jet-setting, living totally from the outside in, never feeling like I was enough, and then I crashed. I became a mom at the height of my career, and realised I couldn't do what I was doing anymore. Burn Out. I couldn't board a plane or a train and had major anxiety attacks. I was in a full-blown identity crisis, searching for my purpose on this planet—or really, for myself. I knew a version of myself, a role I played, but that was not me. It was scary, but the biggest chance of my life to turn everything around.

I knew that in order to create the life of my dreams, I had to become a person that I respect, that feels enough, and loving, because everything is inside out. Our life is a projection of ourselves. And how should I be respected by others if I was rejecting myself?

So I went to work. I studied with every success, high achievement, mindset, energy, and healing coach I could find. I shed my skin like a snake, transformed my shadows into light, awakened to a fulfilled and warm-hearted, very powerful me, and created a life that I never thought was possible.

I created my soul business that's entirely built on purpose and values and love, the extension of my new identity. AND: I know I'm not special. I know you can do all of that too. With this power hack below, I created powerful results, and I can't wait to share it with you now so you can make these shifts too.

So, are YOU ready to shift, so that you can live the life you deserve as the person you love and respect, showing up confidently in this world and achieving your goals with ease? Are you ready for the full version of yourself?

The Identity Shift Ritual

Best is to do this over the next 21 days, twice a day, in the morning and evening. Second best is either morning or evening, and third best is whenever you can. A little trick is to set your alarm on your phone so you won't forget. All you need is yourself, a quiet room, and three minutes for the exercise. Set your timer now and let's begin.

Step Into The WOW-State Step-By-Step

1. **Firstly - Sit up or lie down**. Whatever is possible and comfortable. Close your eyes and take three deep breaths into your nose and out through your nose.
 - Breathe in. Breathe out.
 - Breathe in. Breathe out.
 - Breathe in. Breathe out.
 - Deepen with each breath, and relax as much as you possibly can: your jaw, your shoulders, your hands, your legs, your feet.

2. **Secondly - Step into the new**.
 - Imagine everything you ever wanted to achieve, and you don't

even need to stress out about knowing exactly what that is. Focus on the feeling when it's done. You've made it happen. Happy, lovable, fulfilled, loving, label that feeling yourself. Step into that scenario as if it was already there.

3. **Thirdly - Embody and shift**.
- Get detailed, and ask questions like:
- Where am I?
- What do I see?
- Who is with me?
- What is part of this WOW state? Feel it, because only with feeling can you create a shift in the cells of your body literally right now.
- Lean into it until your alarm goes off.

Train this 'state of being' for at least 21 days. See what happens. It's really just training, because it fires up the wires in your brain, and creates new neural pathways inside of you. The more you practice, the more you become that.

I hope this identity shift serves you as much as it served me. Always know that transformation is the most wonderful gift you can give yourself. I'm very grateful you're doing this work for a thriving self, and ultimately this planet.

Enjoy this new you!

The Time Poor Series: Mindset

About me

Hi, I'm Hedi. I'm a coach, author, motivational speaker, founder of the Hedi Schaefer Academy, a mom and a lover of life. I've been in the coaching industry for over 12 years and support people becoming unapologetic powerful people with a mindset of "yes I can" and a clear strategy on what their purpose, values and visions truly are. Because these are the gaps when it comes to truly successful and long lasting transformation and innovation.

Hedi Schaefer

WOULD YOU LIKE TO FIND OUT MORE?

www.timepoor.me

Notes

The Time Poor Series: Mindset

Chapter 20

Art for Mindfulness?
Tori Press

I'm here to talk to you about one of my favourite ways to take 5 Minutes for Me.

I'm an artist now, but I haven't always been one. In fact, I only started drawing cartoons in my mid-thirties, as a way of finding a personal creative outlet for myself at a time when I really needed one. Since I started drawing cartoons, I've discovered that art is an incredible tool for practising mindfulness, for taking time out for yourself or giving yourself a little me time, and for revealing what's going on inside of yourself (revealing your feelings and your emotional state). I am, to this day, often extremely surprised by what comes up for me when I draw. Maybe you will be, too!

To get started drawing, you don't need very much at all. Blank paper is fine. Anything to write with will do. It can be a pen. It can be a pencil. I have kids, so I'm always getting into my children's art supplies and borrowing their markers. In fact, my very first watercolour set was a Crayola palette that I borrowed from my kids just to try, and found out that I fell in love with it.

Find a quiet spot for yourself to relax and to draw.

The number one piece of advice I can give, is don't worry about what you draw.

Don't worry about what anything looks like.

Don't give yourself this sort of self-talk that I did to myself for very many years, saying that art is only for people who are practiced, who are good at it, whose images come out exactly the way they plan to every time.

I've been doing this professionally for several years now, and things still don't come out the way that I want them to - much less every single time. That's part of the process and accepting that art turns out the way that it wants to is a really wonderful method to learn some lessons in and of itself.

If you need ideas to get started drawing, you can try drawing something abstract and free form.

Just let your hand move across the page in any direction it wants to take.

You can play music and try drawing whatever images or colours come into your mind as you listen.

Another way I love to draw, and one thing I used often to prompt myself when I was getting started, was to find a favourite quotation. Write it out and doodle anything, any imagery that comes to mind from that quotation, anything that you want to embellish it in the margins.

It doesn't matter what comes out. You're just doing this to relax. So, whatever is in your heart is wonderful and fine.

I like to watch the way that lines and colours bloom across my paper.
I like to think of art as a mindfulness practice.
I like to feel the tension in my hand and in my arm as I draw.
I like to feel the way my hand moves across the paper.
I like to consciously try to relax my body even as I work.
I notice if any judgments come up about my work, which they almost always do. Things like; this is good, this is bad, this isn't what I pictured, I hope nobody else sees it. Just watch whatever judgments arise in your mind. Don't try to get rid of them. Don't try to pass them away. Just watch them. Remember, this is about taking some time for yourself. It doesn't matter how it turns out.

Even with only five minutes, you have time to create something that is unique to you, and that only you can create: something that is a unique expression of your individual soul. I encourage you to give it a try the next time you have five minutes for you.

Tori Press

About me

I'm Tori Press, the artist behind the popular Instagram account @revelatori, and the author of I Am Definitely, Probably Enough (I Think) and How to Feel Better: A Hands-On Companion for Getting Through Tough Times. I draw about mental health, self-love, and the vulnerable side of life as a human being.

Tori Press

WOULD YOU LIKE TO FIND OUT MORE?

www.timepoor.me

Notes

The Time Poor Series: Mindset

Chapter 21

Brain Tumours, Basketball and Getting Where You Want to Go
Barry Maher

A cancer doctor I know has a motto posted in her waiting room. Coming from her, it's as profound as it is simple: "He or she who has the most fun wins."

If you can't find joy in whatever it is you're doing, maybe it's time to find something else to do.

Finding Fun in Everyday Life
That's easy for me to say I've got a good life. I talk for a living, which isn't too hard. A while back though, I was speaking on a three-week Asian cruise. Tough gig, right? However, as the cruise

was nearing its end, I was still having trouble finding my cabin. So much so that it became a running joke among the stewards and myself. Then one day I got so lost in the crew section that I almost missed a session.

During my last presentation, I was standing on stage and looked up at the clock. I could see the clock clearly and I could make out the hands. No problem. Only I didn't know what the hands meant. I had no idea what time it was. Not good. I guessed wrong on the time and ended the session fifteen minutes early.

Once I got home. I was suddenly putting my T-shirts on backwards more often than not, and never even noticing it. When I somehow managed to put my pants on backward, my wife insisted I see a doctor.

The Shocking Diagnosis
The first thing the doctor did was have me draw a clock face showing ten minutes past three. The second thing he did was take away my driver's license. I didn't even know doctors could do that. He ordered an immediate MRI. The nurse there wouldn't tell me the results, but she also won't let me use the bathroom by myself, which is something I've always been pretty good at doing.

She said, "Your surgeon will be here in a few minutes."

My surgeon? I didn't even know I had a surgeon. I didn't have a surgeon when I came in. Then the surgeon shows up with three other doctors. There's a whole crew. I thought, maybe they didn't let anybody around there use the bathroom by themselves. I had no idea what the deal was.

My surgeon told me I had a brain tumour the size of a basketball. Or maybe he said baseball. I wasn't tracking too well at that point. By the way, it was possibly, probably (they weren't quite sure) cancerous.

Reflecting on Life and Regret

If you're 35, 45, or 55 and filled with regret about the chances you've let slip by in your life, imagine what life will be like in ten or twenty years, and what you would give then for the time and opportunity you have right now. Or imagine the day when someone tells you that you have giant brain tumour.

As my cancer doctor says, "he or she who has the most fun wins!" I was lucky. My tumour was treatable, and now I'm fine.

Making Life Fun

Let me leave you with a saying from Zimbabwe. If you can walk, you can dance. If you can talk, you can sing. Dance. Sing. Think about working to make your life fun and making it fun for the people around you. Sure, you're anxious to reach your long-term goals, whatever they are. But the more enjoyable you can make that journey towards those goals for yourself and the people around you, the more likely everyone is to be able to sustain the effort it takes to get there.

If you're not enjoying your life now, how long are you planning on waiting before you start?

About me

I'm the author of books like *Filling the Glass: The Skeptic's Guide to Positive Thinking*, and *No Lie: Truth is the Ultimate Sales Tool*. You might have seen me on the Today Show or on CNBC, or speaking for a company you work for, or an association you belong to.

Barry Maher

WOULD YOU LIKE TO FIND OUT MORE?

www.timepoor.me

Notes

The Time Poor Series: Mindset

Chapter 22

Mindset Matters During Menopause
Megan (Mimi Moon) Hayward

Welcome to Peri Earth! As in the wonderful land of perimenopause. I've harnessed a positively charged mindset 99.9% of the time during my menopause journey, and I want you to as well.

I'm the world's first Meno Concierge®, helping women navigate their menopause journey through movement, mindset, and modify® practices. The more women we bring together to raise our voices, share our stories, share our experiences, and our solutions about the menopause change, the better.

I had never even heard the term perimenopause until I was at least two years into my own personal experience, and because I was not aware of the distinction between perimenopause and menopause, I continued to suffer in silence and to be misdiagnosed. My perimenopause started at 38, perhaps a year or so before. I hit many brick walls that were completely unexpected. I struggled with everything because I had fallen into the 20% of women who will have symptoms so severe that they dramatically impact your life.

My menopause journey started, like most women, with a change in my menstrual cycle. However, after experiencing almost all the 40-something symptoms in a short period of time, being diagnosed as seriously iron deficient and advised that I shouldn't be driving, and that I could have bowel cancer, I became depressed. You can read my full story on my website.

What I realised on my darkest days, was that there is a light in all of us. We need to find that and harness it, every way we can, and live our life as positively charged as possible.

Mindset during menopause is really important because with so many changes going on, it can be overwhelming. For me, mindset is more than just positive thoughts. Mindset is about intentionally surrounding yourself with positivity. I worked hard on a few key mindset practices that I've found helpful, and that I think you should try.

First, simply being mindful and fully aware of what you're doing, and focusing on one thing, and one thing only, the present situation at a time. It sounds harder than it is, but if you start by making a list, and actively working through it, one thing at a time, you will stay present and mindful.

Next is chromotherapy—bright, cheerful colours will make you happy. Wearing colour and surrounding yourself with it is a celebration, an announcement of life, positivity, and optimism. Bringing colour into your life, however you choose to do it, will improve your thoughts and influence everyone who encounters you.

The Time Poor Series: Mindset

Try putting a bright paint sample of yellow on your laptop, in your field of vision, and see how your communication becomes sunny.

Use crystals and gemstones to heal and shift energy. Start small. Start with your intention and pick the crystal that your intuition guides you to, the one that you have a strong feeling about, or simply the one that is most visually appealing. Your own body and intuition know what they need, so you will be amazed once you put it out there what comes your way. Personally, I have the vibration of Garnet and Clear Quartz on me and my desk every day, and a huge rock of Rose quartz at my front door. Passionate, motivated, balanced, amplified, loving, loved, kind. Feel it!

Gratitude and Generosity, for me, go hand in hand, or as I like to call it, Gigi. Taking a moment to notice and acknowledge the things you are grateful for each day is strongly and consistently proven to brighten your worldview. Being generous, giving good things to others abundantly, whatever that is, and always paying it forward is equally important. The positive vibrations given and received are backed by scientific research. Try smiling at a stranger, or giving a compliment to someone you see in the street. Both are free and will have a double positive impact.

When you feel stuck, it can be easy to get into a negative thought pattern with negative self-talk. So, say a positive affirmation, chant a positive mantra, or quote. When you repeat a mantra, the sounds echo inside you and carry a positive electromagnetic vibration to your thoughts and your body. "I can, I will, fulfill my dreams". Say that three times and you will feel the positive vibrations inside.

Finally, try meditation. When I first started doing meditation, my mind went everywhere, so I was recommended Deepak Chopra. I find his guidance and voice soothing, and I love how he takes you on a journey back to your centre.

Like most things' menopause; it usually takes a combination of practices to have a positive mindset. Your menopause journey is going to be so much better if you can be a positive thinker. Make the best out of every situation. Focus on what you can control and let go of what you cannot, and find ways to improve each situation and the lesson to learn. Remember that positively charged objects attract each other, so be that positive object! Please reach out to me via my website if you would like more information on how to have a positive mindset, especially as you navigate your menopause journey.

Sending positive vibrations to you all.

The Time Poor Series: Mindset

About me

With a successful career in the property industry, my personal journey through perimenopause ignited a mission to bring visibility to a subject too often kept in the shadows. Initially attributing my symptoms to stress and burnout, I faced years of misdiagnoses before uncovering the true cause: perimenopause.

Today, I speak with passion and authority on the untold realities women face every day and how we can take charge and change the conversation around menopause. I highlight the critical intersections between menopause, divorce, and the housing crisis, emphasising the alarming rise in homelessness among older women.

Through Mimi Moon Meno, I coach, do public speaking, and lead transformative workshops for organisations, empowering women to reclaim their health and voice during this life stage. My mission is to challenge the stigma, elevate awareness, and advocate for systemic change, ensuring that no woman has to face this journey alone.

Megan Hayward

WOULD YOU LIKE TO FIND OUT MORE?

www.timepoor.me

Notes

The Time Poor Series: Mindset

Chapter 23

4 Dimensional Parenting
Tim McCarthy

I'm here to help parents who don't understand what in the world their child is thinking. Does that sound like you? Whether you have a brand new infant and you don't understand why she's crying, a defiant adolescent who thinks he knows everything, or any problem child in between.

Understanding is the first step.

You need to realise that there are four dimensions to human development: The physical, mental, emotional, and spiritual.

We have bodies that need to move and get proper nutrition.
We have minds that need to think and learn.
We have hearts that need to feel and love, and
We have spirits that need something to believe in and to do good.

Western education focuses only on the mental dimension. Four dimensional parents help their children grow in all four dimensions. When you understand how each of these four dimensions develop and the stages they go through as your child matures, you're better equipped to deal with your child as he acts out, while he's trying to figure out how the world works, and you're better prepared to be the guide he needs. You have to understand him at his own level and communicate back at that level to be effective.

The next step is to engage your child in activities to help him reach new milestones in each of the four dimensions.

For example, if your child has trouble dealing with emotions, I have a little game called I'm Going to Be. The first step is to help your child understand what he is feeling. A young child doesn't know his emotions yet, so you name it to tame it. "Oh, are you feeling sad?" And he learns what sad feels like. The next step is to teach opposites. "What's the opposite of sad?"
"Happy!"
"What's the opposite of angry?"
"Calm."

Once you have established that baseline of emotional knowledge, you play the game like this. "I feel sad, but I'm going to be . . ." and wait for your child to fill in the opposite. "I feel angry, but I'm going to be . . ."

And then when you notice your child feeling sad or angry, you ask, "How do you feel?" When he says, "Sad." You counter with, "But I'm going to be . . ." and let him fill in the opposite. This little game teaches him to learn how to change his emotional state.

To help a slightly older child deal with spiritual or moral decisions, offer some situations and discuss them like, "Your best friend asks you for the answers on a test. What do you do?" Or, "You see your friend steal a candy bar in a store. What do you do?" Of course, after she answers, you would ask, "Why?" and discuss the reasons. An important next question might be, "What else could you do?" to develop a growth mindset.

Unfortunately, we don't have time to go into more depth, but I have hundreds of activities like these in my book *Raising 4 Dimensional Children in a 2 Dimensional World*. If you want to become a four dimensional parent, pay attention to your child's needs in each of the four dimensions. Understand where he is and what would be the next step, and then help him take those next steps.

About me

I have a master's degree in education with years of experience as a classroom teacher and administrator in both public and private schools, and a grandmaster rank in the martial arts with even more years of experience teaching and developing martial arts programs. This background gives me a unique perspective in balancing Eastern and Western theories of education.

Tim McCarthy

WOULD YOU LIKE TO FIND OUT MORE?

www.timepoor.me

Notes

The Time Poor Series: Mindset

Chapter 24

I Can Do This
Joanne Greene

Like so many, I was a person in constant motion, anchoring the news and hosting talk shows on San Francisco radio for decades. While totally devoted to my family, nothing would slow me down—not even losing my mother, my sister, and my brother in a four-year period. Nothing, until I was hit by a car as a pedestrian, and suddenly, I found that I couldn't do anything, not even get myself to the bathroom.

Circumstances can crush us, make us crumble, freeze us in our tracks, or lead us to give in to self-pity. Or we can use the challenging situations in which we find ourselves to spur personal growth. I'm not saying it's easy, only that it's an option. We can't control what happens to us, as much as I had always tried, but we do have a say in how we respond.

My first reaction upon realising that I'd been hit by a car was to silently scream. Really? The subtext was, haven't I been through enough? Now this? My next thought was, okay, let's do this. Now, I'm not sure where that strength came from, but I grabbed it like a brass ring as I was determined to survive. "I can do this" quickly became my mantra, and it sustained me through five excruciating days in the hospital and the next year plus, as I recovered from the trauma and major injuries, which included four pelvic fractures. I got through the long days of pain, immobility, and flashbacks by, among other things, counting my blessings.

I may be in pain, but at least I didn't have a serious head injury. I may not be able to feed myself, but at least I have a husband who's taking care of me. When I was younger, I had rolled my eyes at that age-old adage, "count your blessings." But this time, I quickly learned that it works. Gratitude beats down despair. It's a law of nature. Another trick was reminding myself of something my mom had always said: "This too shall pass." The thing is that no matter how bleak life looks at a given moment—when you're having a setback in your recovery, for instance, or you wake up from yet another nightmare in a cold sweat—it's helpful to tell yourself that this is a moment. It won't always be this way, that change is inevitable, and that the next moment or tomorrow you will feel something different. You may even feel better.

Unable to be productive in the ways I'd previously chosen to fill my time—like working, cooking, cleaning, or writing thank you notes—I finally learned to meditate. Five minutes for me. See? You're already on your way. For years I'd tried and given up because my mind just kept on racing. Turns out that meditation is called a practice because that's what it takes—tons of practice. Now, years later, I meditate regularly.

It's a tool that I rely on to keep me calm, more centred, and less reactive. Things will happen to all of us in life, and it makes an enormous difference when one has a community to call upon. Thankfully, I did, and people showed up selflessly to walk our dog, deliver dinner, and stay with me in the early days so that my husband could periodically get a break. I vowed to always leave time in my schedule to show up for others, to text and call when people are suffering—not to ask if there's anything I can do, but to say that I'm bringing a meal and ask what their dietary restrictions are. Few of us are comfortable asking for help, but most of us appreciate the opportunity to help when someone we know is having a hard time.

In June of 2023, I published By Accident: A Memoir of Letting Go, which chronicles my journey after the accident and over the next few years, when I had more opportunities to employ what I had learned. By Accident is available in paperback, as an audiobook, and an e-book. Read it for inspiration. Maybe buy it for a friend who's struggling. We cannot control our lives, but we can control how we react to the failures, breakups, injuries, illnesses, and losses that we face. Post-traumatic growth is achievable. In fact, our greatest personal growth is often available in times of transformation.

Joanne Greene

About me

Joanne Greene never bought the adage "little girls should be seen and not heard." She's used her voice on San Francisco radio and television, webinars, and podcasts, to explore the issues of our time with playful irreverence, candor, and compassion. Now, with many decades of seasoning, she's sharing what she's learned about navigating family and career, moving through pain and loss. Follow her podcast, "In This Story...with Joanne Greene" on all major podcast platforms.

Joanne Greene

WOULD YOU LIKE TO FIND OUT MORE?

www.timepoor.me

Notes

The Time Poor Series: Mindset

Chapter 25

What is 'realistic optimism' and how do I cultivate it?

Peta Sigley

Have you ever wondered whether it's truly possible to maintain a positive outlook in the face of life's (often seemingly endless) challenges?

Realistic optimism is a mindset that integrates hopeful expectations with a pragmatic view of challenges and setbacks. It's an approach that can enhance our emotional wellbeing and enable us to navigate both our personal and professional lives more effectively.

Based on principles of positive psychology, realistic optimism fosters a balanced perspective that recognises both the potential for positive outcomes and the realities of life's ups and downs.

Practicing realistic optimism can transform your approach to obstacles, making you more resilient and hopeful. Unlike delusional optimism, which ignores potential risks and challenges, or pessimism, which dwells on negative outcomes.

Realistic optimism acknowledges difficulties but approaches them with a hopeful and constructive attitude. An example of realistic optimism is "today's a challenge but tomorrow will be a better day when we do x, y, z". This can be compared to the response of a delusional optimist who might ignore risks and say, "everything is fine, it'll be ok" or a pessimist who might think "today's a challenge and tomorrow will be worse; I can't cope".

Realistic optimism requires ongoing effort and attention, but with commitment, you can develop a mindset that helps you to cope with challenges and thrive in the face of adversity.

Applying realistic optimism involves integrating these principles into everyday situations. Whether managing personal relationships or professional responsibilities, maintaining a hopeful yet grounded outlook fosters resilience and enhances problem-solving abilities.

So, how do you cultivate realistic optimism in your life?

Take decisive action
Face difficult situations head-on with a positive mindset. For example, if you need to have a tough conversation, approach it with the belief that addressing issues will lead to constructive outcomes and long-term improvements.

Communicate openly
Build trust and strengthen relationships by communicating transparently with those close to you. Openly discussing challenges and sharing information fosters a collaborative and supportive environment where everyone feels valued and informed, deepening

mutual understanding and connection.

Maintain your focus
Minimise distractions and negative influences. Focus on what you can control to stay grounded and productive in both professional and personal endeavours. Breaking down larger tasks into smaller, more manageable steps helps maintain clarity and reduces feelings of overwhelm, enabling you to achieve goals more effectively.

Practice resilience
Incorporate resilience-building wellness practices into your routine. Taking regular breaks, prioritising self-care, and managing stress effectively not only benefits you but also sets a positive example for those around you.

Practice mindfulness
Reduce stress and remain present through mindfulness and meditation techniques. These practices can help you manage emotions, enhance concentration, and make more thoughtful decisions in challenging situations.

Stay connected to your purpose
Reflect on your values and align your actions with them. Understanding your core values provides a compass for making decisions that resonate with your beliefs and goals.

Celebrate small wins
Acknowledge and celebrate achievements, no matter how small. Recognising progress, such as completing a difficult task or reaching a milestone, boosts morale and reinforces a positive outlook on future challenges. Sharing these successes with others creates a sense of camaraderie and collective optimism within your community or team.

Realistic optimism is not about denying challenges but embracing them with a belief in your ability to navigate and grow from them. By integrating positive expectations with realistic assessment and proactive coping strategies, you empower yourself to thrive in both personal and professional domains.

Embrace realistic optimism and experience the power of balancing hope with reality. Your future self will thank you.

About me

My name is Peta Sigley and I am the CEO and Co-founder of Springfox, Australia's leading providers of evidence-based resilience training for individuals and organisations. I have a background in psychology and education, and over 20 years' experience working extensively with individuals, teams and organisations to help build resilience and enhance performance and wellbeing – both inside the workplace and outside it.

Peta Sigley

WOULD YOU LIKE TO FIND OUT MORE?

www.timepoor.me

Notes

The Time Poor Series: Mindset

Chapter 26

Building a bulletproof mindset
Luke Kingston

Today, I want to thank you for investing time in yourself, and I'm eager to share this moment with you as we explore the crucial elements of developing a bulletproof mindset that will stay with you throughout your life.

First, let's tackle something that frequently holds us back: limiting beliefs. These are the nagging thoughts that whisper we're not good enough, smart enough, or capable of achieving our dreams. The truth is, these beliefs are merely stories we tell ourselves. To build a bulletproof mindset, we must identify and challenge these limiting beliefs. Replace "I can't" with "I can," and transform "I'm not good enough" into "I am enough."

Now, let's discuss the importance of becoming comfortable with being uncomfortable. True growth occurs when we venture beyond our comfort zones. The most significant experiences often lie just past the edges of familiarity. Embracing discomfort means facing challenges head-on, understanding that it's ok to stumble, and recognising that failure is simply a stepping stone on the path to success.

Do not fear discomfort. Embrace it, for it is where the magic happens.

Discipline serves as the bridge between goals and achievements. Building a bulletproof mindset requires developing self-discipline. This means setting clear goals, creating a plan, and sticking to it, even when you don't feel like it. Discipline fosters consistency, which ultimately leads to success.

A healthy lifestyle is another vital component of mental resilience. Nurturing both body and mind through regular exercise, a balanced diet, and sufficient sleep significantly impacts your mental well-being. When you're physically healthy, your mind is better equipped to handle stress and adversity. This is a powerful aspect of a bulletproof mindset.

Remember, building a bulletproof mindset is a journey, not a destination. It's about challenging limiting beliefs, embracing discomfort, practicing discipline, and maintaining a healthy lifestyle. These principles aren't just abstract concepts; they are actionable steps that can transform your life. The mind is like a muscle—the more you work on it, the stronger it becomes.

So, embrace the discomfort, stay disciplined, and take care of your body and mind. Your journey to a bulletproof mindset begins today. I hope you can embark on this transformative path with determination and resilience!

The Time Poor Series: Mindset

About me

I am many different things to many different people—a brother, a friend, a coach. But what sets me apart is what I stand for. I place a heavy emphasis on self-development, growth, and discovery. I challenge myself daily through my dedication and commitment to martial arts and fitness, always seeking new skills and knowledge while pushing my limits through challenges and competitions. I do this while staying true to myself and spreading positivity to everyone I meet, encouraging those around me to become more fulfilled versions of themselves. None of this would be possible without my relentless work ethic. I aspire to get better every day, and my discipline and sacrifice have resulted in the creation of my coaching business, which is committed to helping you build a bulletproof mindset while becoming self-aware.

Luke Kingston

WOULD YOU LIKE TO FIND OUT MORE?

www.timepoor.me

Notes

The Time Poor Series: Mindset

Chapter 27

Fear Journaling
Joel Evan

I am so excited to share with you this idea of fear journaling. I don't hear a lot of people talking about this. I hear a lot of people talking about gratitude journaling or writing down their affirmations and their visualisations. Don't get me wrong, I like all of those things and I do all of them. I think they all work. But I think something that's missing, and integral for a lot of people, is this idea of fear journaling.

Now, here's the thing. I lost my job during the pandemic. I was a first responder for over 14 years. Then out of nowhere, lost my job during the pandemic. I had to pivot. I had to do something different. As a matter of fact, we moved out of state. We started a whole new life. I had to now do something radically different, get out of my comfort zone, be decisive, and take action. I was scared. There were a lot of times I just didn't know what was going to happen, or what I was going to do. I was lost, and I was in this state of overwhelm and fear-stricken. I didn't know what to do.

I started fear journaling, just really writing down everything. You can either write it out, or you can voice record yourself. Just write down your biggest fears.

By the way, just a little helpful pointer. You want to do this before you do any type of gratitude work, and we can talk more about that. But here's the idea: you need to get your fears out of your head in order to allow you to move forward in a stable manner.

It is kind of an emotional colonic is the way I describe it. If you think about this, if you're letting a bunch of stuff hang out in your subconscious and you keep walking around, blocking the stuff out with all this positive thinking, you're just going to continue to feel bloated. You're going to continue to feel bloated, and still in the background are these crappy feelings.

So, by getting all your fears out, especially the really big ones, and when you actually put them on paper, you finally will allow space and positivity, and innovation and faith to flow through you. Get out those bad fears, and make room for your subconscious for the better.

Here's the thing that I always notice. When I actually get these things, these fears out, and I keep doing it day in and day out until finally I wake up in the morning, and I just don't feel anything, I don't have any emotional charge. The fears are just gone.

What I notice is, when I get them written out onto paper, when I see them very clearly, a lot of times, the fears, the things that are causing this overwhelm and preventing me from taking action and preventing me from moving forward, they're not really that scary after all.

I start to get a lot of clarity. I start to really see them for what they are. I'm like - Oh! If I just do this one action step, all these things and all my fears will go away.

Everything is going to get better.

So, one of the questions I like to ask myself is, what would I do if I didn't fear anything?

Or, what's the worst that could really happen?

Getting clarity, and starting to see what these fears are really about, has allowed me to move forward in this time of the unknown when I didn't really know what I was going to do.

Remember, if you start to feel overwhelmed, which I think a lot of times is where our fears stem from, just say thank you, and be gracious about what has happened.

Because if you're in a state of overwhelm, it actually means you have more than enough. You have so much that you're overwhelmed, and you don't know what to do with it, so just give thanks.

Lastly, one of the things I mentioned earlier was, don't do gratitude work before you do your fear work. It's impossible to be grateful for something and at the same time have anger and fear. That's why I think a lot of people do too much gratitude work, and don't spend enough time with their fears. So, when you're having these emotions of fear or anger, it's impossible to just pretend that everything's all good and great.

Do your fear work, and then do the gratitude exercises afterwards. Because if you don't, all you're going to do is be putting a sticker on, or covering up those fears. You're not going to really replace them with gratitude. So, unless you get the fears out, the gratitude work will not be as powerful.

What would be in your Fear Journal?

About me

I am an integrative health practitioner, life coach, and host of The Hacked Life podcast.

Joel Evan

WOULD YOU LIKE TO FIND OUT MORE?

www.timepoor.me

Notes

The Time Poor Series: Mindset

Chapter 28

Change Your Thinking to Change Your Life
Victoria Gregg

You can transform your life by shifting your thoughts. If you are ready to take the steps to recreate yourself and reclaim your life - Where should you start?

Well, your mind is the perfect place to start.

Your perspective and mindset are critical. When I studied people who had transformed their lives, they all spoke about how they changed their lives by changing their thinking. Wayne Dyer said, "If you change the way you look at things, the things you look at change." This is such an important concept, and it's one that's worked for me in my own life and with my clients.

Mindset and perspective significantly impact how we redirect our thoughts. Listening to negative people or watching the news can make us more cynical. Negative bias is the tendency to focus more on adverse events than on positive ones.

When I'm working with a client, and I'm going to do a happy childhood regression with them, they often say, "I'm afraid that I don't have any happy memories from childhood." Ultimately, discovering joyful memories they forgot about changes their whole perspective on their childhood. The pleasant memories then trigger more of the same. Afterward, they mentioned that their early years may not have been as awful as they remember.

The negative things that happen to us have a more significant impact on our lives than the positive ones, and we feel them more intensely. When you turn on the television and see the doom and gloom being broadcast, it brings in ratings, but it can cause us to become disillusioned and stuck. It also puts us into a state of fear. It isn't easy to explore how we can shift our circumstances when we are in that state. Your life won't evolve if you don't go outside your comfort zone. You can't keep repeating the same patterns and behaviours and expect a different result.

A negative mind will never give you a positive life, so be careful who and what you allow in it. Remember, your diet is not just the food that you eat. Your diet is everything you ingest and absorb into your mind, body, and spirit. It's watching the negative things on television. It's what you read. It's who you allow to have access to you.

Pay attention to the people in your life that either drain or elevate you. Maybe you've gone out for lunch with a friend or family member, and afterward, you were left feeling depleted because they complained the whole time, and their grim mood brought you down. Be careful of those people. Shut out the negativity. Focus on yourself. Go within and discover what you want in your life and what you don't by closely evaluating it.

When you start your day with positivity, you will notice that you can navigate unfavourable situations smoothly. You can't be optimistic if you wake up and the first thing you do is put on the news or start complaining. Instead, focus on the blessings in your life. Try to spend five minutes outside having your coffee, listening to the birds, or playing music. You can then retrain your mind to focus on the good. We've been programmed to look for the bad in situations. There will always be less-than-desirable situations, but how you let them affect you is the key to transforming them.

If you do not like your path, get off of it. Start by taking baby steps. Then, you will have the stamina to focus on and obtain your goals. When people make their goals too lofty and expect them to be accomplished quickly, they often give up on them prematurely.

If you are going to climb a mountain and you're standing at the bottom of it looking up, it seems like such a daunting task. But if you break it down by concentrating on the first quarter of the mile, then the next half, and the next mile after that, it becomes like a game, and you will begin to become inspired by your progress.

Go slow, start small, and have patience. Remember, you have to expect setbacks and failures. But setbacks are just a recalibration, and failures are lessons. So, remember, you are not forced to stay on the trajectory you're on right now. Set out in the direction that you want to go. Focus on your desires and make your dreams happen.

About me

Victoria Gregg is a transpersonal hypnotherapist, holistic life coach, speaker, and writer. With a rich twenty-five-year background in healthcare, she boldly transitioned to a new career in her fifties, fueled by the courage to leave a toxic relationship and the desire to live life on her own terms.

Victoria Gregg

WOULD YOU LIKE TO FIND OUT MORE?

www.timepoor.me

Notes

Chapter 29

Mindset Secrets of Police Officers and Navy Seals for Civilians

Matthew Dickson

I've got schizophrenia. I'm doing well now, but it took a while to get here in my recovery, and I read many books and had to get myself better.

There are a few books that really stood out to me. One is called "Verbal Judo: The Gentle Art of Persuasion" by George Thompson, and it teaches people how to deal with others with words, not weapons. It's what police officers use. They're trained in verbal judo, and it's helped me immensely in dealing with people. Number one is to stay calm.

So often when we have someone speak to us with harsh words, we rise up and match back with harsh words. Try to stay calm. When you stay calm, it's more likely that the other person will come back down to your level. A lot of people, as they say in the book, haven't been heard, seen, or acknowledged, and they're stressed and just want someone to listen to them.

Can you be that person for someone, to stay calm and just let them vent? Most violence that a police officer would come across can simply be talked through. That's been a great help for me.

Also, one of the main things that they teach in verbal judo is to talk from their frame of reference, not yours. Find out where they are.

Where are they mentally?
Do they need a hug?
Are they listening to you?
Are they upset?
Where are they?

Find out where they are, and you have to be able to read body language and have emotional intelligence to do this. When you do that, when you find out where they are, you talk from their frame of reference.

So often, I'd walk into a room and start talking about what I had to say, not paying attention to where everybody else in the room is, and it's been such a great help.

The third thing of verbal judo is to just stay calm and let them de-escalate and calm back down. Stay calm, find out where they are, talk from their frame of reference, and just help de-escalate the situation. Just let them vent. That's been a huge help to me.

Another book is "The Survivor Personality" by Al Siebert. He documented for decades how people got through the Holocaust, natural disasters, cancer, and alcoholism. He studied how people got through it, flourished on the other side, and thrived. That's been a real help for me.

Another book is "Unbeatable Mind" by Mark Divine. Mark Devine is a Navy SEAL. He's trained thousands of Navy SEALs, and he teaches the mindset secrets of Navy SEALs in his books. His best book for mindset is "Unbeatable Mind." It's helped me immensely. Navy SEALs are taught in their training that you are capable of 20 times more than you think you are.

In their training, they're taken to the brink of physical and mental exhaustion and they say, "I can't go another second, I quit, I give up," and they're shown in their training.

They are spoken to at that moment and told, "You think you're done? Not only do you have double what you think you've got, not just 5% more or 10% more, not even 100% more. You've got 20 times more than you think you do." I was shown that in my recovery from schizophrenia. It's very difficult. But I did it, and I got through it. It's possible. It seems impossible. It seems like you can't go any further. But you can. You do have that inside you. And I believe everyone has that.

It's remarkable what the human body and the human mind can go through. Those are some of my top tips and I hope that's of some help to you. I've got mental illness. I know how badly the mind can go. If you're fighting, if you're struggling with your mental health, if you want to improve your mindset, please keep fighting. There's always hope. Life can be very difficult, but just keep fighting, keep hoping, and don't give up. It's well worth it.

About me

I'm a mental health advocate and a schizophrenia advocate. I help people with mental illness in developing countries get access to basic mental health care. I'm sharing insights to help you improve your mindset. You can find out more www.MindAid.ca

Matthew Dickson

WOULD YOU LIKE TO FIND OUT MORE?

www.timepoor.me

Notes

The Time Poor Series: Mindset

Chapter 30

High Performance
Gavin Freeman

For me, the difference between good and great is the ability to perform consistently under pressure, and that's where I spend my time working now with elite athletes, elite businessmen and women, and organisations in looking at how they can perform effectively under pressure.

I've always been fascinated by human performance and how we get the best out of ourselves. I've looked around to try to understand why some individuals are simply the elite of the elite and questioning, how do they do that? Are they any different?

What I've found over the years is that actually they're not. In fact, every one of us has the potential to be an Olympian, the potential to be a world champion, the potential to be at the top of our game. But it's the methodology we use, it's the way we train, it's the way we develop that is crucial. I've picked up a few nuggets along the way that have helped me not just understand it, but share it with others to help them on their journey to achieve whatever goals they're trying to achieve.

Breaking Self-Limiting Beliefs
Many people, when they reflect on their ability to perform, often start with a self-limiting belief system. "I can only go this far. This is as good as I'm going to be. I'm only going to be a manager. I'm only going to be an executive. I'm only going to be a CEO. I'm never going to be a board member."

So, I think we all start with a little bit of self-limiting belief and where that comes from. Look, it stems from a whole variety of different places: our education, our upbringing, our cultures.

When we look at the elite of the elite, they don't have that. They don't have that self-limiting belief. They look at a situation and it's no longer a problem, it's simply a hurdle. It's about how we get over those hurdles. Most people start at that point. Then they explore outwards and say, "Where could I go?" Again, we see another bit of self-limiting belief systems kicking in, saying, "Well, I can't play in this space or I can't play in that space.

It might be because I'm too short, I might be too small, I might have the wrong body size or shape, I might not have the right background or education." Then we start to unpack that and look at other experts and what they've done.

The Role of Motivation and Resilience
We start to recognise that it's less about who we are, the size we are, the colour of our hair, our educational background. It really comes down to our motivation to succeed, how driven we are to

succeed, and more importantly, how we deal with failure and our motivation to avoid failure.

Within that construct and that continuum, I always like to explore those motivations to help individuals break through their own self-limiting beliefs.

The question around sport and business always comes up, and often business looks to sport and puts them on a pedestal to suggest how wonderful these individuals are. What I've found over my career is the correlation and the similarities, and it's less about the physical performance. For me, it's all about the mental focus, the perceptual ability, motivations. In fact, what we find there is that the correlations are incredibly high.

While many senior managers, executives, workers, even grads coming out of university may not profess to have the physicality of elite athletes, what we can develop is that mental focus and mindset.

That's where I see a huge opportunity: understanding the way we think, understanding the way we make decisions, being able to make decisions with a lack of information or time, which are often characteristics athletes have to deal with.

Parallels Between Sport and Business
They don't know what the opposition is doing, they don't have enough time because the clock is running down, and they don't have all the information because they may not be able to see where their teammates are behind them.

It's about how we can make some of those decisions, and there's a high parallel in business. We've got to make decisions quickly, we don't always have the information, we don't know what our competitors are doing, yet we want to stay ahead of the curve, be innovative, and be progressive in our nature.

I think there's a lot we can learn, and athletes have developed skills that I see corporate individuals using every day, developing those skills every day. For me, it's a very high correlation.

What I was saying before, it's that self-limiting belief system. There are a couple of factors that play into that as well. There's also the belief that if I just try harder, I will be successful. That's an absolute no-no. Trying hard doesn't equate to success.

The final piece of the puzzle is the way I try. Most people will do simple repetition, they'll try something and practice it over and over again, then wonder why they're not getting better at it.

My very simple analogy is you and I have been walking all of our lives, yet we're not better walkers than when we first learned to walk. From ages three to seven, we don't get better; in fact, we get worse at walking because we're walking all the time. We tend to stumble and trip over now, whereas learning a skill is not just about learning the knowledge of the skill, it's about putting it into practice and being able to respond. For me, it's that self-limiting belief, then it comes down to not trying hard; we need to be clever in the way we try. The final piece is that we've got to have a very deliberate learning style to truly achieve our goals.

About me

I'm a sports and corporate performance psychologist, I spent nearly 15 years with the Australian Olympic team, working with high-performing individuals, helping them achieve their potential and helping them perform under pressure and a further 15 years transferring those skills into the corporate world.

Gavin Freeman

WOULD YOU LIKE TO FIND OUT MORE?

www.timepoor.me

Notes

Notes

Notes

Notes

Notes

Notes

Notes

Notes

Notes

Notes

ACKNOWLEDGMENTS

Thank you to all of the wonderful authors who joined in bringing this book to life, we are forever grateful and could not have done it without you!

Scott Greenberg	1
Cathy Jimenez	7
Mark Zimmermann,	11
Dr Anneline Padayachee	19
Veronica Llorca-Smith	25
Tony Ryan	31
Stuart Taylor	37
Michael Crossland	43
Irenee Brooks	49
Cristina Dovan	55
Rik Schnabel	61
Jem Fuller	67
Gail Gibson	73
David Penglase	79
Anthony Ikin	85
Dr Helena Popovic MBBS	89
Sinead Sharkey-Steenson	95
Darren Fleming	101
Hedi Schaefer	107
Tori Press	113
Barry Maher	119
Megan (Mimi Moon) Hayward	125
Tim McCarthy	131
Joanne Greene	135
Peta Sigley	141
Luke Kingston	147
Joel Evan	151
Victoria Gregg	157
Matthew Dickson	163
Gavin Freeman	169

www.ingramcontent.com/pod-product-compliance
Lightning Source LLC
Chambersburg PA
CBHW061735070526
44585CB00024B/2686